A U.S. Army Soldier's Cold War Memoir
1970-1973

Michael W. Heyer

Copyright © 2021 by Michael W. Heyer

All rights reserved. No part of this publication may be reproduced, distributed, or transmitted in any form or by any means, without prior written permission of the author.

Publisher's Note: Some names and identifying details of people described in this book have been altered to protect their privacy.

Book Layout © 2017 BookDesignTemplates.com
Cover Design © 2020 Elizabeth Sarrazin

A U.S. Army Soldier's Cold War Memoir/ Michael W. Heyer. -- 1st ed.
ISBN 979-8-7334726-7-6

Front cover photo of a Pershing 1a missile with live warhead sitting in its cradle at Kleingartach Combat Alert Site (CAS).

Back cover photo of a Pershing 1a missile with live warhead sitting in its cradle at Kleingartach Combat Alert Site (CAS).

Dedicated to my late wife Janet Murphy Heyer who saw something in me, and my life was never the same thereafter.

CONTENTS

Disclaimer i
Preface ii
Prologue 1
Chapter One – The Mart Building, St. Louis 3
    Enlistment and Induction 3
Chapter Two – Fort Leonard Wood, Missouri 9
    Reception Station 9
    Basic Training 12
    Yes Sir 24
    Push-Ups 24
    Marching 25
    Rifle Ranges 26
    Policing the Grounds 29
    Shots and Injections 29
    Weekend Passes 30
    Sick at Christmas (1970) 31
    Final Testing 32
    Graduation 33
Chapter Three – AIT (Advanced Individual Training) 35
Chapter Four – Fort Dix, New Jersey 40
Chapter Five – Germany 42
Chapter Six – Badnerhof Kaserne, Heilbronn 44
    On Duty 54
    Tracking Time 55
    Organizational Chart 55
    Superiors/ Commanders 58

Battery Commanders 58
Top 58
Motor Officers 59
Motor Sergeants 60
Military Driver's License 62
Transfer To Commo Platoon 63
Working on Vehicles Could Be Dangerous 65
Bearing Issues with the M757's and Trailers 66
Vehicle Identification 67
Operational Status and Lack of Parts 68
New Toolboxes 70
Kidder and the Logbooks 71
Birthday Celebration 72
Army Training 72
Inspections 73
Music 75
M16 Annual Re-Qualification 78
Alcohol and Drugs 78
Murder 80
Alcohol, Drugs, and Me Personally 81
Promotions 83
Patches, Medals, and Other Awards 84
CQ Duty 88
Maneuvers 89
Europe on Red Alert 90
Leave 91
Article 15 92
A New Shipment of Heaters 94
Peewee 94
Motor Pool Buddies and Others 97

Surprise Practice Alert	101
New Jeeps	101
Food Runs	102
Enlisted Men's Club or NCO Club	102
Borrowing Money From Guys	103
Calling Home	103
Mail Call	103
Television	106
Stars and Stripes	106
Snack Shack	107
3 Coin	107
Missile Launch	107
Salty Language	109
German Language	109
German Weather	110
Mercedes 230 SL Convertible	111
Captain Spencer	112
5/4 Ton Accident	114
1972 Olympics	115
A Ghost Story	116
Chapter Seven – Kleingartach, Germany CAS (Combat Alert Site)	118
Pershing System Cycle I	121
Pershing System Cycle II	121
Pershing System Cycle III	121
The Guard Shack and Major Kelley	126
KP (Kitchen Police)	127
Missile Trailer Issues	128
Volunteering	130
Head Injury	131
Williams and Omelets	132

Battalion Commander's Helicopter 133
Harrison's Car 135
Fatal Auto Accident 137
F4 Phantom Jets 140
A Sunday Walk in the Forest 141
Chapter Eight – Neckarsulm Kaserne, Neckarsulm, Germany 143
Ammo Dump and Guard Duty 143
Gun Incident 144
Out of Uniform 145
Moving to Neckarsulm 146
A Fire in the Barracks 146
The Hesters Living on the Economy 147
Commissary 147
Maneuvers 148
Chapter Nine – Wharton Barracks, Heilbronn 149
Chapter Ten – Redleg, CAS/ Training Site Outside of Heilbronn 151
Picnic 152
Maneuvers 152
Shorty and the Glow Plug 153
Chapter Eleven – Grafenwoehr (Graf) Training Site 155
Souveniers 159
Chapter Twelve – Vehicle Trips and Mishaps 160
Hood Mishap 161
Babich's Accident 161
Crossing the Highway 163
Heilbronn's Narrow Back Streets 164
Connors and a Stop Sign (Halt) 164
2-½ Ton Truck with Rear Axle Knocked Out of Alignment 165
Rolling Truck and a German Shed 166
Road Trip to Ramstein 167

Breakdown on the Autobahn 168
A New Wrecker 169
Our VW Bug 169
The Generator Incident 170
Transported by a Chinook 171
Tragic Loss 172
Chapter Thirteen – Heilbronn, Germany – The Town 174
Oktoberfest 174
The Western Store 175
Rock Concerts in the Park 175
Volksmarches 176
The World's Oldest Profession 177
Working at the Local VW Dealer 178
German Movie Theater 179
Black Market Purchase 180
Chapter Fourteen – Auto Racing 182
Kidder and Shorty Racing Team 182
Hockenheim Races 183
Nurburgring Grand Prix 183
Le Mans 184
Chapter Fifteen – Stories After Rotating Back to the States 188
A Thanksgiving Feast to Remember 188
Racial Tension 188
CQ Duty Again 189
Hester and Captain Spencer (Battery Commander) Meet Again .. 189
Deadly Accident 190
The Cost of Getting Mixed Up with Drugs 190
Chapter Sixteen – Rotating Back to the States 192
A Gift 192
Going Home 193

- Returning to Civilian Life 194
- Visiting Heilbronn in 1997 195
- Making a Home in Europe 196
- Stress on the Job 197
- Speaking with High School Kids 197
- Other Connections 199
- On the Other Side 200
- Loss of a Pioneer 200
- Defcon 3 201

Chapter Seventeen – End of the Pershing Missile Program 202
- 2010 Reunion 205

Epilogue 207
Postscript 208
Acknowledgements 210
About the Author 211
Bibilography 213

DISCLAIMER

I have made reasonable attempts to be as accurate as possible with my dates, descriptions, places, individuals, and all other content within this memoir. However, this past October 2020 it was 50 years since I enlisted. As such, I'm rather certain some of my recollections may contain errors. Regardless, I have tried to convey the spirit of my time in the Army, the places I served, and the fine men with whom I had the honor to serve. Note: there were no women in Pershing at that time.

    I obtained approval to use actual names of those mentioned in this memoir and images of Army buddies where possible. If I was unable to obtain approval, I changed their name.

    All photos are the property of the author unless otherwise noted. Fort Leonard Wood photos on pages 11, 12, and 14 are public domain. The M16 photo on page 23 is public domain. The map on page 43 is courtesy of Google Maps. The C5 Galaxy photo on page 109 is public domain. The VW engine photo with Kidder on page 114 and the wrecker photo on page 136 are courtesy of Barry Kidder. The F4 Phantom Jet photo on page 141 is public domain. The M60 Patton Tank photo on page 157 is public domain. The Chinook photo on page 173 is public domain. The back-cover photo of a Pershing 1a is courtesy of Walter Gates.

PREFACE

I did not keep a daily journal during my time serving in the military. At the time, I believed that only girls kept such a thing. Regret is too strong a word to use, but I do wish I had kept one. The time spent serving my country would eventually have a profound lifelong positive impact on me. As such, I have decided it is time (since I enlisted 50 years ago last year) for me to attempt to document as much as I can recall from that time in my life.

PROLOGUE

Ernest Rutherford performed the first artificially induced nuclear reaction (splitting an atom) in 1917.

The Manhattan Project began on August 13, 1942. It was a research and development undertaking during WWII with the specific goal of producing an atomic bomb.

The first detonation of a nuclear device (informally named "The Gadget") took place on July 16, 1945, at 5:29 a.m. at the Trinity Site, New Mexico. It measured approximately 22 kilotons.

It has been stated the 20th Century Nuclear Arms Race began during talks with our allies (Great Britain and Russia) after VE Day regarding the status of the war with Japan at Potsdam, Germany on July 24, 1945, when Stalin (who secretly already had knowledge of the U.S. atomic development program [i.e., the Manhattan Project] because of a spy in the program) was informed by Truman the U.S. had an atomic bomb. Truman did not know that Russia was already in the process of developing an atomic bomb as well.

The North Atlantic Treaty Organization (NATO) was formed in April of 1949. The organization's primary goal was "to keep the Russians out, the Americans in, and the Germans down."

In January 1958, the Department of Defense (DOD) announced a new solid-propellant missile had been developed and was named Pershing in honor of General of the Armies of the United States John J. (Blackjack) Pershing.

Construction on the Berlin Wall began on August 13, 1961.

The first Pershing missile (P1) fielded by the U.S. Army in West Germany was in 1963.

The P1 was upgraded to the P1a in 1970.

CHAPTER ONE
THE MART BUILDING, ST. LOUIS

ENLISTMENT AND INDUCTION

I enlisted in the U.S. Army on October 26, 1970, when I was only 18. It was a little over two years after the Tet Offensive in Vietnam, the assassinations of both Reverend Martin Luther King Jr. and Senator Robert F Kennedy, the Democratic National Convention riots in Chicago, and President Lyndon Baines Johnson stating he would not seek a second term. The reason for Johnson's decision not to run was because he had lost the confidence of the American people resulting from the Vietnam War. Also, it was one year after President Richard M Nixon took office, the National Guard shootings killed four students at Kent State, Neil Armstrong and Buzz Aldrin from the Apollo 11 crew landed on the moon and safely returned to earth, and Woodstock (three days of peace and music) happened. And finally, a few months after the ill-fated Apollo 13 mission (called a successful failure) took place. Certainly, a turbulent time in history.

My draft number was in the upper 200's, so I would not have been drafted. I had graduated the previous May from St. John Vianney High School, an all-boys school in Kirkwood,

Missouri. In August of that year, I started at Meramec Community College also located in Kirkwood, Missouri, because at that time I was totally unclear as to what I wanted to do with the rest of my life.

I now realize I was more than likely learning disabled (LD) and had problems with auditory processing. Such learning problems had not yet been identified in the education system along with other disorders and thus were unknown at that time. That coupled with the fact that I was now attending a co-ed school was too much for me. I was flunking out right away and recognized I needed to do something else. So, after about one month at Meramec, I quit. I can be guilty of impulsivity and began thinking about joining the military. But I also knew that I could not continue to live off my parents. Besides, their marriage was in shambles and that just added to the problems (they eventually separated within a year of my finishing my tour and eventually would divorce). Something had to change.

After visiting the recruitment office located on Gravois Road in Affton, I decided to enlist in the Army. I considered both the Navy and Air Force, but both required a four-year active commitment and that seemed like an eternity. The Marines just were not on my radar at all because I knew that if I joined the Marines I would more than likely have been shipped off to Vietnam.

In the Army, you could enlist for two years, but it was common knowledge at that time that if you enlisted for two years you would more than likely be sent to Vietnam upon completion of all your training. However, if you enlisted for three years of active duty you could request your assignment. As such, I enlisted for three years with Europe as my first choice and the United States as my second choice. Note: all enlistments were for six years. Whatever was not as active status would be completed as inactive in the Army Reserves. I signed up around the end of September with a commitment date for the end of October. By the time I enlisted, opposition to the Vietnam War was very high.

I broke the news to both my parents later that day and we all cried. It was not easy to tell them, but I knew it was the right decision for me.

I was required to report to the Mart Building in downtown St. Louis (at that time located next to the St. Louis City Police Station) first thing Monday morning on October 26, 1970. I said goodbye to my parents and ex-girlfriend, Donna (she had broken up with me the month before, which was the right thing to do because we were so young at the time), and we all cried together before I was off to check-in.

Upon entering the building, I stepped into a world I could not have imagined. The building was full of military personnel, doctors, and those of us who were there to be processed (those that enlisted or were drafted). While waiting to begin the induction process, I befriended Jackson (in the military we always went by our last name), a guy from Dupo, IL, and would end up going through basic training with him. He had signed up to attend Cryptography School at Fort Monmouth in New Jersey after Basic Training. I assume he ended up at Fort Meade and would guess he either made the Army a career or worked in cybersecurity.

Once the process began, the first thing we had to do was receive a complete physical. All of us were required to strip, leaving only our shoes, and stand in line for several hours of prodding, poking, and being asked a series of questions about our health. It was quite demoralizing, to say the least. Later I would come to realize this was the military's first chance to take away our individuality, which would continue throughout basic training and even occur to some degree during AIT (Advanced Individual Training).

After the physical portion of our testing was complete, we began taking various psychological and intelligence tests. Once all testing was complete, I was approached by an officer to ask if I would have an interest in attending the Military Academy at West Point. To this day I do not know if everyone was approached or if I was singled out because of my test results. I declined because at that time it was not on my radar to go to college or to make the military a career.

By the end of the day, we had completed all necessary testing, review, questions, etc., and were now escorted into a room where there were approximately 30 of us. We were told that we were about to take an oath to serve our country and to defend the Constitution of the United States. It was made clear that once we took this oath, we would officially become a member of the military and there was no backing out. No one declined and we all raised our right hand. The oath I took is as follows:

The Oath of Enlistment (for enlistees):
"I, _____, do solemnly swear that I will support and defend the Constitution of the United States against all enemies, foreign and domestic; that I will bear true faith and allegiance to the same; and that I will obey the orders of the President of the United States and the orders of the officers appointed over me, according to regulations and the Uniform Code of Military Justice. So, help me God."

We must have had dinner at some point, but I do not recall it. We were then escorted to board a Greyhound Bus. We had no idea where we were going but eventually ended up on I-44. By then it was dark, and I could see the lit highway signs and lights through each of the towns as we drove southwest. Late that evening we arrived at Fort Leonard Wood (named after the Army Doctor who identified how workers were contracting Malaria during the construction of the Panama Canal and who is later credited with developing a vaccine).

At the time, Fort Leonard Wood was the largest Basic Training Facility in the U.S. Army covering over 61,000 acres and with up to 5,000 trainees at any given time going through training. It was home to the 5th Army and included Engineer Training and an Engineering Unit and Mechanics Training School as well.

CHAPTER TWO
FORT LEONARD WOOD, MISSOURI

RECEPTION STATION

The first place we went to was called the Reception Station. By then we were all exhausted and taken to a large room where drill instructors informed us that this was our last chance to turn in any contraband items such as knives, drugs, girly magazines, etc. that we may have brought with us. After that, if you were caught with any of those items you would be in serious trouble. Interestingly, as they passed around baskets to collect these items, some guys had actually brought contraband and were quickly disposing of it. I could not believe guys had brought stuff like that with them. After what seemed like a very long time, we were taken to an old WWII barracks, assigned a bunk, and went to bed. I bet I fell asleep in less than a minute.

For the next five days, guys would continue to arrive as the Army was in the process of accumulating enough GI's (government issue) to form a company. During those five days, we were kept busy. We received our first military-style haircut. The barbers used electric clippers to cut our hair very short – we were not allowed to have any type of facial hair during training either. We were measured and distributed our military gear:

boots (two pair), dress shoes, rain boots, five sets of fatigues, a fatigue jacket, poncho, mittens with a trigger finger, head covering that could be worn under your helmet and could wrap around your face (we called it a snoopy hat), leather gloves with liner, helmet liner, helmet, class A uniform (including a dress coat and two dress hats), boxer shorts, T-shirts, and socks. Once in uniform, our rank was E1 (enlisted 1). I learned the hard way why we were issued boxers when I wore briefs one day as we marched to the rifle ranges. By the time we returned to our barracks that evening I was completely chaffed from wearing briefs. I never wore them again during Basic Training.

Each of us was issued a duffel bag that had our full name and service number stenciled on it. An interesting fact is that our service number at that time was our Social Security Number, which would not be a good thing in today's electronic world. We were also issued a set of dog tags that contain the following information: full name, service number, religious affiliation, and blood type. You are issued two tags so if you are killed in action one is left with your body and the other is taken by another soldier for reporting purposes.

We were also issued the materials needed to assemble half a pup tent. The other half was carried by your partner. We were issued a gas mask, backpack, ammo belt with ammo packs, medical packs filled with medical supplies, canteen, a mess kit, and a sleeping bag. Since I wore glasses, I was eventually issued glass lenses that were inserted in my gas mask because a gas mask will not seal properly if you are wearing regular glasses.

Around this time, a photo was taken of me and I was issued my active military ID card. Unfortunately, that day I happened to have a huge pimple on my cheek that was quite prominent. That photo would be my only form of identification for the next three years.

As all of this occurred, we marched everywhere singing a variety of different songs with the cadence of the drill instructor. As we were learning to march, the drill instructors were quite nice to us and never yelled. Little did we know that was about to change.

Exterior of WWII barracks used for the reception station and AIT living quarters.

Interior of the same barracks pictured above. We had rows of bunk beds rather than single beds as pictured.

BASIC TRAINING

Basic Training consisted of a wide array of training and drills. Here are just a few items that I'll cover below: M16s, wide-open rifle ranges, automatic firing range, night vision rifle range, qualifying rifle range, disassembling and cleaning your weapon, hand grenades, bayonet practice, gas masks and tear gas, claymore mines, Belly crawling for 100 yards at night with machine-gun fire overhead and surrounding mortar explosions, first aid, topographical map reading, compass reading, calisthenics and physical fitness, confidence course, overnight bivouac, C rations and bad tasting coffee, KP, guard duty, so many inspections, marching everywhere, educational movies on frostbite, trench foot and how to avoid flipping jeeps, running a mile, passing physical tests, etc. All of which was done in the winter, regardless of what the weather might be like outside.

Basic Training consists of eight weeks of intense physical, weapons, and many other forms of training. Our military-issued weapon was the M16 and we learned very quickly that it was always referred to as a weapon. If you referred to it as your gun, the drill instructor would yell back at you that it was your weapon and that your gun was part of your male anatomy.

Friday morning arrived at the Reception Station and boy did the climate change. The drill instructors flipped on the lights at dawn and began yelling at us to get all our gear packed in our newly issued duffel bags and to line up outside as quickly as possible. I assume everyone was as scared as I was. When we went outside, we stood lined up in formation by several deuce and a half's which are actually 2-½ ton troop transport trucks. We were instructed to toss our gear on the back of a truck next to us. Whether we moved quickly or not, the drill instructors yelled at us to toss our bags quickly and then for us to climb aboard quickly as well.

Keep in mind, drill instructors have a very tough job. They are responsible for turning a bunch of green recruits (civilians) into soldiers and they only get eight weeks to accomplish that task. I'm sure it must have been in the back of their mind that some of the guys they were training could end up in Vietnam and never make it back home again. In retrospect, it seems like a daunting responsibility.

We then made the short drive – probably about 15 minutes – to what would be our home for the next eight weeks. We pulled up in front of newly constructed barracks that appeared to be a few years old, three stories tall, modern, and constructed of brick.

Built in the 1960s and the type of building I lived in during basic training.

Again, the drill instructors began yelling at us to grab our gear and disembark as quickly as possible. I ended up in a second-floor dorm room with guys whose names also began with "H". The room more than likely slept about eight guys and was on the rear right side of the building. We each had a bed, a footlocker, and a wall locker which can best be described as a metal armoire. Our gear, two storage areas, bed, room, floor, and various other rooms were to be kept immaculate.

Right away we were instructed on how to make our bed with "hospital corners." If our bed was not made correctly or the way the drill instructor liked it, he would mess it up and tell us to do it again. Each of us had an assignment that was performed every morning before chow. All these chores needed to be completed every day: windows and windowsills wiped clean; floors swept, mopped, and then buffed; bathrooms cleaned; showers cleaned, and washbasins cleaned. Again, each task had to be performed until the drill instructor was satisfied. Even if it meant repeating the same task.

In addition, we were required to dress in a clean and neatly pressed fatigue uniform, and our boots were always to be polished. If we returned from an outing that got our boots dirty, we were required to clean and polish them that night.

Inspections in the military are a way of life and we were constantly going through one kind or another. Besides inspecting our personal area, common areas of responsibility, personal hygiene, uniform, and our weapon, on occasion we had inspections of our wall locker and footlocker as well. Everything had to be hung or folded in a certain way. We also had inspections for our ammo belt and related gear. All of it had to be laid out a certain way on our bed. If we did not have it set up correctly, we would have to do it again until we passed. Another example of the level of perfection required was part of our uniform. Our uniforms contained brass insignias and a brass buckle. When issued they had a lacquer finish to prevent tarnishing and the first thing the drill sergeant did was to make us rub off that protective finish. That way he could easily tell if we hadn't polished them.

It should be noted that sometimes guys would not shave as was required daily. If a recruit was caught unshaven, the drill instructor would keep a razor handy and have the offender dry shave right there on the spot. Doing so would result in irritating the skin leaving a razor burn.

At that time, there was a risk of contracting viral meningitis, a highly contagious and sometimes fatal disease. As such, as part of our bed making, we were required to use one of our tent poles and a pillowcase to create a double triangular shaped shield at the corner nearest the bunk to us and located at our pillow end. We were also required to sleep with the windows slightly open so fresh air could enter the room. During Basic Training five guys contracted the disease, and I believe of the five, one of them died and at least one became seriously ill and almost died. So, the risk of contracting the disease was very real.

My first night in Basic Training at Fort Leonard Wood just happened to be Halloween. That evening after a very eye-opening day I went to dinner with my new friend Jackson. As we were walking back from chow towards our barracks, we both began to cry. Remember, we were both just 18, had enlisted for three years, and did not know when we would see our loved ones next. As we both cried, we couldn't help but ask each other what kind of hell we had gotten ourselves into. Little did we know this was just the beginning of our military experience!

From time to time throughout Basic, AIT, and Germany (my permanent station) I would get very homesick. I guess it was just part of growing up.

I remember there was a time when two of my friends got into a fight in the barracks, Holiman and Harry. Holiman was from Santa Barbara, California, and used to jump on his footlocker and pretend to use it as a surfboard. He told us he used to surf all the time back in California. Harry was from St. Louis and was sometimes challenged by the physical activity requirements. Well, Holiman used to relentlessly tease Harry about his challenges and at one point it was too much for Harry. He jumped on Holiman and began wrestling with him. I do not recall any punches being thrown and at some point, someone stepped in and broke it up – one of the older guys in charge.

During the next eight weeks, we would learn many new skills and get into excellent shape. Part of our morning routine before breakfast each day was calisthenics. We went through a variety of exercises designed to build our strength for all the physical activities we would be required to perform. In addition, we spent a good deal of our training at the rifle ranges. And there were several different ranges designed to address specific types of weapons training.

During our training, we learned how to read topographical maps, which would come in handy as we would need to be able to determine the terrain of where we were in any given location/situation.

We would learn how to disassemble our weapons, clean them, and then reassemble them, performing all steps quickly, about a minute to break it down and another minute to reassemble. We cleaned our weapons every night after returning from the rifle ranges before they were returned to the armory where they were stored in a secure vault in the basement.

We also learned how to use our weapon as a club. We did so by fighting one on one with Bunge Sticks. We would wear a helmet and groin protection and then fight in an enclosed area until one of us scored enough points to beat our opponent.

Gas mask training was a required element of Basic Training and involved instruction on how to adjust our mask so it would not leak. Then we were escorted into a small, enclosed building approximately 12' by 12' in groups of 10 and once inside we were exposed to tear gas. The first step was to give a thumbs up to our drill instructor to ensure our mask was sealed properly and that we could breathe without any restrictions. Once that was confirmed, we were instructed to remove our gas mask and were not allowed to leave the building until we inhaled the gas. As soon as each of us inhaled, we began choking and everyone scrambled for the door. Once outside, we continued to cough as our eyes, nose, and throat burned like hell.

Just in case anyone had a serious problem there were a couple of medics on call at the site. I do not recall anyone feeling that bad, but it was a very unpleasant experience.

Anytime we ate– breakfast, lunch, or dinner – we were divided into three lines: RA (Regular Army), AR (Army Reserve), and NG (National Guard). Each evening after completing a day of training I was so hungry I began to eat food I would never have eaten previously. An example is baked beans. Before serving in the Army, I disliked them and would never eat them. That changed and today it is one of my favorite foods. There was, however, one food I could not bring myself to eat: liver and onions. It was the only time in Basic Training that I left anything on my tray.

Something else related to eating that I was able to experience once or twice was KP (kitchen police). We normally rose at 0530 each morning during Basic Training. However, when assigned to KP we had to be up by 0430 to assist the kitchen staff. We worked the entire day until late into the evening long after dinner was over. We washed pots and pans by hand, ran trays, glasses, and utensils through the dishwasher, cleaned tables, emptied trash cans, hand-peeled potatoes, etc. I remember being completely exhausted after I finished my shift. Since we were just trainees, the cooks could be very hard on us.

Another form of training we received was the art of throwing or tossing live grenades. There was a specific site we marched to for this exercise and once there, we were instructed on how to crouch into the proper position and toss a grenade, keeping our arm locked, throwing it over our head into the designated detonation area. A grenade is not thrown like a baseball. There were approximately three or four staging areas with a concrete floor and concrete wall about four feet high on three sides. Each of those areas had one trainee and one drill instructor. Those who waited their turn or who had finished waited in a long underground concrete bunker. Obviously, all of this was for safety reasons should someone be careless enough to drop a live grenade. The explosion created by each grenade was very loud. After I threw my two grenades, I peered over the side of the wall to see the detonation area full of craters. It was quite an interesting experience, to say the least.

On another day we were trained in hand-to-hand combat. We marched (as always) to a large building that was filled with about a 12" layer of sawdust and spent the day learning how to grab someone lunging at us and flip them over our shoulder. We practiced it until we could do it correctly.

Another training day was spent learning how to properly use our bayonet, which was attached to the end of our weapon. This particular training site consisted of dummies (simulating a body from the waist up) attached to ropes at the top and bottom. There were probably a half dozen with enough space between each one so we could thrust our bayonet into the dummy then run to the side of it and attack the next row of dummies.

During our time in Basic Training, we also had to march several miles to an area where we would spend about 24 hours outside on a bivouac (temporary encampment). We were paired up with another guy before assembling our pup tent. It was a very cold night to sleep in tents and there was a dusting of snow that covered everything when we awoke the next morning. I also remember a mess truck arriving to feed us a hot dinner using our mess kits, but that breakfast and lunch consisted of eating unheated C-rations. And with each C-ration pack, there was a small device called a P38, a small can opener used to open the C-ration cans. I kept one and still have it to this day.

Sometime during our training, we viewed a movie on the danger of contracting frostbite and trench foot. Frostbite occurs when the skin on your extremities such as fingers, toes, ears, or nose freeze. There are differing degrees of severity, the worst being when the frozen portion of your body essentially dies, and you lose it. Trench foot is similar, but it occurs when you spend too much time standing in water. As a result, your feet rot and they need to be amputated. This occurred primarily during WWI because most of that war was fought in trenches. It was a graphic film showing the severe damage that can result from either condition. Obviously, it was designed to scare the hell out of us, so if we ever found ourselves in such a situation, we would do everything possible to prevent it from happening especially changing our socks regularly. The movie sure scared me.

Another film we were required to watch was how to correctly steer a jeep back onto the road if it veered off onto a soft shoulder. They have a high center of gravity and as such roll over more easily than other vehicles. I know of at least one instance in Germany where a guy overturned a jeep and was killed while attempting this type of maneuver.

We also learned about claymore mines, a type that is buried in the ground. When it exploded it would generally blow off the legs of the unfortunate soul who stepped on it if it did not kill them. These were used extensively in Vietnam.

We were also taught basic first aid where we learned how to set a broken arm or leg and how to dress various types of wounds. It was very interesting to participate in these types of training.

On another day, we had to navigate the confidence course which consisted of an elaborate maze of obstacles that we had to cross and confirmed the excellent shape we were now in. I loved doing physical training like this as it took coordination and stamina, and I found it to be a fun activity.

Probably one of the most interesting exercises we had to complete took place during the evening hours at a unique course. It was about 100 yards long (at least it seemed like it was that far) and we were marched to the far end of the course where we waited in a long, deep trench. At the other end, there were a half dozen 60-caliber machine guns in fixed positions. In between was a course that required us to crawl on our belly (low crawl) the entire length of the course while navigating obstacles such as barbed wire, craters, telephone poles lying on their side, etc. Within the barbed wire areas, explosions were set off simulating incoming mortar fire.

As we crawled through this maze, machine guns fired approximately three feet over our heads, and to assist us with seeing what was happening above our heads, every fifth round was a tracer (an iridescent projectile). It was quite an experience. The idea is to simulate what it feels like to be in a combat situation including being shot at. I don't think anything can prepare you entirely for real combat and someone trying to kill you, but this is the Army's attempt to do so.

Of all the training we received, the longest and most intense training was firing our M16 under a variety of different settings and conditions. The M16 I used (photo below) consisted of the following specifications:

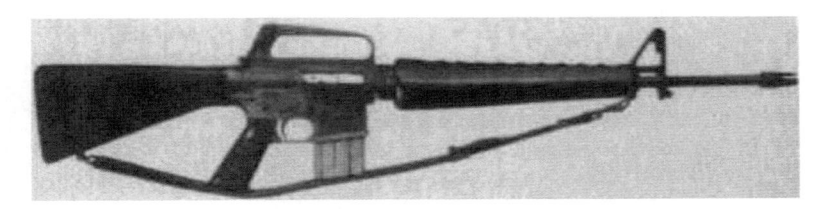

Weight loaded:	8.79 pounds
Length:	39.5 inches
Clip:	20 rounds
Cartridge:	5.56 X 45 mm
Muzzle Velocity:	3,110 feet per second
Effective Range:	601 yards
Maximum Range:	3,937 yards

For the most part, we marched several miles to the rifle ranges, spent the entire day there, then marched several miles back to our barracks at the end of the day. When we returned in the evenings, we were required to disassemble our weapon and clean it before dinner.

YES SIR

One of the mistakes all new recruits make is to address your drill instructor as "sir." However, generally one makes that mistake only once. I did so and was quickly admonished for addressing an NCO (sergeant) as sir. I was informed that sergeants work for a living and that only officers are addressed as sir.

PUSH-UPS

During basic training, you do lots of stupid things such as calling your drill instructor "sir" or getting out of line for one reason or another. Anytime you do so the drill instructor's solution to the problem is to make you do push-ups. There were several occasions where my drill instructor got frustrated with me about something and would say "drop and give me 50" – meaning 50 pushups. After a while, they get to be rather easy because you are doing them so often.

MARCHING

As previously mentioned, we marched to and from the rifle ranges most of the time (a few times we were transported back in trucks). However, we marched everywhere. I always felt sorry for the guys with short legs, because we were all supposed to step out 36" heel to toe, so we all kept the same uniform stride. Whenever I talk about all the various forms of training we received, we marched to that training and back. Sometimes we marched with our weapons, sometimes with full gear on our backs. Other times, we just marched as is. Always marching. And most of the time we would march to the cadence of the drill instructor. I recall two songs specifically that we marched to often. One was titled "Vietnam" and mentions the Vietcong and Charlie in the lyrics. We would sing it to the music of "Poison Ivy" a 1950's song I always liked. I specifically recall part of the lyrics – "late at night while you're sleepin' Charlie comes a creepin' around!" The other song we marched to was "We Gotta Get Outta This Place" by The Animals.

Marching consisted of learning how to march in step with your unit. We learned how to march forward, do an about-face, and march in the opposite direction. How to march to the left as a column, to the right as a column, quick time marching, and half time marching. An interesting fact is that marching in unison always ceases when going over a bridge. That is because marching in unison can cause a harmonic vibration that can cause a bridge to fail.

However, before we could learn to march as a unit, we first had to learn the basics. How to stand at attention, how to stand at ease (parade rest). We learned how to perform an about-face, how to do a right face turn, and a left face turn.

We also had to learn how to properly salute. You salute with your right arm. The index finger should be touching the corner of your eyebrow fingers together hand facing downward. The forearm should be at a 45-degree angle with the ground and your upper arm should be parallel with the ground. A salute should be snappy and deliberate.

RIFLE RANGES

We spent the bulk of our rifle range time at a range that had various distances for the targets. Initially, our first time out we had to sight in our weapon which means we had to adjust the site by firing at a target 50 yards away. Adjusting the site consisted of making small changes to affect the direction of the projectile.

There are two adjustments to be made – windage and elevation. Windage determines whether the projectile travels more to the left or the right. Elevation obviously determines the up and down direction of the projectile. We would keep firing and adjusting until we were hitting the target consistently where we wanted to. After that, we spent a great deal of time taking our turn shooting at targets (upper half of the body) at various distances: 50 yards, 75 yards, 100 yards, 150 yards, 200 yards, 250 yards, and finally 300 yards (three football fields). There were probably 15 – 20 trainees on the firing line at any given time when given the ok to fire when ready. All the while drill instructors paced behind us, observing what we were doing. If someone got careless and pointed their weapon in any direction other than downrange, they would get chewed out severely. And regardless of whether the weapon was loaded, you were taught to ALWAYS treat it as if it were – NO EXCEPTIONS! During this time, I would venture to say we fired hundreds if not thousands of rounds to become proficient with our M16. At the end of basic we would be tested on how proficient we had become. We were trained in various positions – prone (lying on our belly), kneeling, and standing.

When not at the firing line we would be in the rear in a large, heated tent trying to get warm or trying to get coffee so we could get warm. Their coffee usually tasted a bit soapy in flavor, and I was never sure if it was on purpose or by accident. Frustratingly, it tasted as though they had not rinsed out the brewing container very well. But when you are freezing you will do anything to try and get warm including drinking lousy tasting coffee. I just loaded it up with a lot of cream and sugar. Eventually, we would be told to get out of the tent because not all of us could fit in there at any given time. I think it was just the drill instructors being drill instructors.

On several occasions, it was so cold my toes would go numb, and that was even while wearing galoshes over my leather boots and wearing wool socks. This was the only other time during Basic Training that I cried - at the ranges. While at these large open ranges the wind would often blow – sometimes very hard because there was nothing to break the wind.

Another range they took us to was the automatic range. The M16 was normally set on semi-automatic, however, it could be converted to fully automatic—a machine gun—with the flip of a switch. At this range we were all issued three full magazine clips, each holding 20 rounds. Our instruction at this range was that we were free to fire those three clips as quickly as we wanted to. It was awesome to fire my M16 in that setting. I more than likely went through my clips in less than a minute, since you could empty a clip in a matter of seconds, pop it out, insert another, and start over.

As part of our weapons qualification, we had to go to the ranges at night. We were taken to a building where they instructed us on how to use our peripheral vision to hit a target in the dark. To hit a target in the dark, you must not look directly at your target, but rather just to the side of it. You are then able to see the target with your peripheral vision. After their instruction, they turned off the incandescent lights and turned on black lights, which allows your eyes to adjust to the darkness. It takes about 20 minutes for your eyes to adjust to optimal night vision. We then went out to a range that had targets located 50 yards away. To qualify, you had to hit the target 10 times out of 20 rounds. I had difficulty hitting the target for some reason but was eventually given credit for hitting my target the required number of times. To this day, I am unclear as to how many times I actually hit the target.

POLICING THE GROUNDS

This was performed everywhere I served. It is a common clean up tactic the military uses. It involves everyone walking abreast in a straight line while picking up trash. However, it goes one step further. We all had to pick up cigarette butts as well. It certainly has the area clean once finished, but it can be a tedious job if smokers drop their butts everywhere.

SHOTS AND INJECTIONS

I remember another occasion where we were being marched to an aid station to receive our injections. We were ordered to strip to our waist and walk through a line of five nurses/doctors to receive five injections at once. I recall three were the old fashion way using a hypodermic needle. However, two of them were administered using a gun. It was not a pleasant experience at all, but I never really minded getting shots. I do recall the guy in front of me started bleeding because the doctor using one of the guns moved it slightly and it in effect cut the guy's skin.

I remember another time when I was not feeling well and was at the aid station to get treatment and was falling asleep in my chair. Some medic thought it amusing to stick smelling salt under my nose to wake me up. It had a terrible odor, and I was very frustrated that he did that.

WEEKEND PASSES

We did not have a lot of freedom during Basic Training. My parents visited me once and they brought my ex-girlfriend (Donna) with them. We went bowling and had a meal at the bowling alley. Later during AIT, we had more freedom. I recall my mom driving down and picking me up a few times. Looking back, my mom was so good to me and always jumped at the chance to help me get home or back to the fort even though I'm sure it was a huge inconvenience for her. But isn't that what parents do for their kids – pretty much anything they need. That is the unconditional love of a parent with their child. During those trips home, I recall the radio was playing songs like "River Deep Mountain High" by The Supremes and The Four Tops, "Tears of a Clown" by Smokey Robinson and the Miracles, and "My Sweet Lord" by George Harrison.

Before that, I actually took the bus home a few times. The first time it took us to the airport, then my mom had to drive there to pick me up. After that, I figured out that if the bus driver pulled off I-270 at Big Bend, I could walk home from there. I did that once or twice. I was so glad to be home even if it was only for about 48 hours.

Once, I found out that a guy stationed at Fort Wood was going to St. Louis for the weekend and was giving rides for $15. I took him up on it. He had a fast Camaro, and a friend was with him. So, during AIT Henning and I rode in the back seat. It was not a wise decision. The passenger in the front was a friend of the driver and after we exited the fort, they began drinking beer from a 6 pack they had purchased at the PX (post exchange) as they drove about 90 mph all the way to St. Louis. I was scared to death and never did that again.

SICK AT CHRISTMAS (1970)

During Basic, we were given a seven-day pass to go home, and unfortunately, I was sick as a dog. Several of us had the flu and we were told that the adult thing to do was to check into the hospital at the fort instead of going home. They must have thought we were stupid. There was no way I was going to check myself into the hospital and miss Christmas at home. When I finally did get home, I slept on the couch for three days. I was literally passed out most of that time. I was so out of it, but so happy to be home.

Fortunately, by Christmas Day I was well. Interestingly, my parents somehow arranged for their family to be the oblation bearers at the 10:00 am service and I proudly wore my uniform.

Little did I know that one of the guys (Dan) who I went all through school with was in attendance that morning. At that time, he was attending the University of Missouri – Columbia and enrolled in the pre-med program. He was one of the "popular" guys in school but was always very nice and friendly with everyone. Dan approached me and congratulated me on joining the Army. One thing he shared with me that sticks with me to this day was that he wished he could have done what I did and enlisted. I never forgot that this guy, who always excelled at everything and was someone who everyone admired, respected something I did.

After leave was over, I returned to the fort along with all the other trainees. We were getting very close to graduation now, which would take place in early January 1971.

However, before we could graduate, we had to pass several tests – physical as well as qualifying with our M16.

FINAL TESTING

Remember we already had to qualify with 10 successful hits at our night-time target. We now had to go to our final firing range. This range was set up for several of us to fire at individual targets at the same time. Each trainee's targets were staggered using the same distances as the open ranges where we spent most of our time during rifle training. However, the difference between this range and the other open range was this one was set up with a more natural forest/jungle-type setting with trees and bushes all around including having the targets located at several different elevations (the range was V-shaped with a valley in the middle). The added level of difficulty was that the targets would randomly pop up at any given moment anywhere within the range and the objective was to hit the target before it went back down. They were not up long at all – maybe 10 seconds. We had 90 rounds to fire on this course. Overall, I ended up with a total score in the range of 80 – 90. At least that is what the award on my uniform indicates which was classified as a sharpshooter. I'll explain all of the rankings when I cover medals and awards later on.

The physical test consisted of completing a course that included disassembling and then re-assembling my weapon within a certain amount of time and various physical challenges and obstacles throughout the course as well. Specifically, one of the physical tests required running one mile within a certain time. Of course, the fact that I smoked didn't help, but I was well within the time required and passed.

GRADUATION

Graduation from Basic Training occurred on a very cold January 8, 1971. I remember my parents were in attendance, but I do not recall if either or both of my brothers were there. We marched along with the other training companies in front of our commanders and all the visitors. It was very gratifying to know I had completed all of the training required of me before moving on to AIT, which for me was mechanic school. The nice part of this for me was that this school was also located at Fort Leonard Wood. The MOS (Military Occupational Specialty) code for me was 63B20 – Tactical Fixed Wheeled Vehicle Mechanic. I received my orders and proceeded to my new assignment.

CHAPTER THREE
AIT (ADVANCED INDIVIDUAL TRAINING)

The barracks where I would live for the next eight weeks were located near the southernmost unrestricted area of the fort (rifle ranges, etc.) in old wooden two-story barracks that had been constructed during WWII. The second floor was entirely open – i.e. one very large room. Bunks were stacked two high and were spaced about two feet apart. This was the configuration on each side of the floor with a long space in the middle that ran the length of the floor. Each bed had a wall locker and a footlocker. The footlockers were stored under the lower bunk.

The lower level had a similar sleeping area however, it also contained a private room for our sergeant, a space that contained sinks, toilets, urinals, and a washer and dryer. It also had a shower room that was one large shower with several showerheads. The noteworthy part of this arrangement was there was absolutely no privacy whatsoever. The toilets were on one side of the room, spaced about a foot apart and without any walls so that anytime you used it you might have someone right next to you or using a sink, a urinal, or the washer or dryer. It was, to say the least, very demeaning. Anytime I had to use the toilet, I would make sure I had a newspaper with me to hold up in front of me. Also, anytime you used the shower room you had to walk through the room containing the toilets, etc.

During AIT we had to stand in formation in the morning and the evening. We also had to march everywhere when going to mechanic school (commonly referred to as grease monkeys). However, overall, we were treated better than during Basic and our sergeant was not as strict as the drill instructors had been. The school buildings were about a ten-minute march from our barracks.

Interestingly, each platoon had a mascot and ours happened to be a bison located in a pen outside our barracks. In retrospect, it was not fair for the animal to be in a pen about 30 feet by 30 feet.

Anyway, mechanics school was eight weeks long. I recollect that training consisted of classroom instruction, then we would practice what we learned on the same part of the vehicle. We learned about repairing and maintaining both gas-powered and diesel-powered engines. We also learned about working on the drive train, including the propeller shaft, brakes, wheel bearings, etc.

We learned about the cooling system, the fuel systems, and the electrical systems. Interestingly, a typical electrical system for civilian cars and trucks is 12 volts. However, military vehicles have 24-volt systems. The two 12-volt batteries were wired together in series rather than parallel.

Another interesting fact about military vehicles is that some were designed to have the intake and exhaust pipes to be located above the cab. This would allow them to traverse rivers or other bodies of water. The electrical systems were also sealed to enable the vehicles to travel through water. The only modification required so that you could drive underwater was to first loosen the fan belt.

Many vehicles also had a transfer case built into the drive train behind the transmission. This would allow for a PTO (power takeoff) shaft to attach to a winch on the front of the truck. The winch is used to pull out trucks that are stuck.

During training, we were taught various tricks or workarounds. One example involves gas-powered engines. A gas-powered engine uses spark plugs and a distributor cap with a wire coming out of it that goes to each spark plug. In the center of the cap is another plug that's connected to a solenoid. Within the distributor cap is a set of points and you have to remove the cap to access the points. The distributor supplies electricity to the plugs at the proper time and sequence to each cylinder and the points assist with this process. However, points must have a gap that is factory specific and there is a tool with various thicknesses so you can properly set the space based on those specifications. In one of the classes, we were taught that if you don't have the tool and are in a pinch you can use the cover of a matchbook since its thickness would be close enough to get you by.

I remember one of our instructors liked to use the word "tendency." For whatever reason, he would often use that word to describe something, such as the distributor cap tends to send electricity to the spark plugs. I was always thinking to myself that this guy did not understand the definition of that word or how to properly use it.

Another funny story from AIT. There was a nice guy who was from a very rural area, who had never owned an electronic device (according to him). So, he was very excited when he bought a battery-powered cassette player. The ONLY tape he had was Johnny Rivers' greatest hits and he played it any time we were in the barracks during downtime – over and over and over again. What really made it fun was that I slept on the top bunk and he slept on the top bunk next to me. I liked Johnny Rivers, but hearing the same tape on repeat was not only driving me nuts but the 40 other guys on the floor, which if you recall was one big open bay. The guy in question was so nice, but he had no clue. And if we brought it up, he just smiled.

One time during AIT, we were marching from one location to another when I was hit in the back of the head with a rock. Someone in the group behind me must have thrown it and I don't know if I was the intended target or if it was someone in front of me. I can't imagine I made someone angry enough to do that to me. Regardless, it hurt, and I was quite angry. And I never did figure who did it.

I completed my mechanic's training in early March (March 8th comes to mind). I remember gathering with all the other trainees in the first floor sleeping area waiting to hear our orders for our permanent assignment. Some of the guys received orders for Vietnam. Others' orders were for various posts in the United States and others either Korea or Europe or some other part of the world. My orders were for Germany and I was very excited that I was assigned my first choice. I was very interested in leaving the country, going to Europe, and experiencing living in another country. I would have a few days at home before having to report to Fort Dix, New Jersey for transfer to Germany.

At this time, there were one or two guys who decided to attend Jump School at Fort Benning, Georgia. I considered it because it sounded like it would be exciting and awesome to learn, even though I did have some fear of heights. The final exam at Jump School was jumping out of a plane five times – then you earned your parachute wings medal. Before that, your final training on the ground consisted of jumping off a 200-foot tower with a parachute. This school was entirely voluntary and lasted for three weeks. The only reason I didn't apply was that I was tired of training and wanted to get to my permanent assignment.

CHAPTER FOUR
FORT DIX, NEW JERSEY

I would spend about three days at Fort Dix. I was there with two guys that I had gone through basic training and AIT with – Henning and Harry – both from St. Louis. Ultimately, I would end up in the same battery with Henning. Harry on the other hand was in the same battalion but would end up in a different battery at different barracks (Neckarsulm Kaserne).

While at Fort Dix, I once had to pull guard duty overnight. I recall having to guard a PX which was like a much smaller version of a Walmart or a Target. Anyway, the night was chilly, and I was required to walk around the perimeter of the building with an unloaded M16. This particular guard duty was for twelve hours with two hours on and four hours off. It was cold and I recall singing to myself to pass the time. The two songs I recall singing were "Leaving on a Jet Plane" by Peter, Paul and Mary, and "The Letter" by The Box Tops.

Henning and Harry in our temporary barracks at Fort Dix, New Jersey. They're standing in old WWII barracks still in use at that time (same as the kind I lived in at Ft. Leonard Wood).

Within nine months of arriving in Germany, Henning was transferred back to St. Louis to work at the Army Depot in Granite City, IL. He was transferred because his father became ill and was unable to work.

CHAPTER FIVE
GERMANY

After about three days, I received orders to proceed to Frankfurt, Germany where I would be processed into the European Theatre. We flew out of McGuire Air Force Base, New Jersey on a chartered jet bound for Ramstein Airbase outside of Frankfurt. From there we were taken by bus to a location in downtown Frankfurt to be processed. My recollection is I was there for just a few hours. We then were taken to the Frankfurt train station, where we boarded a train bound for Schwabisch-Gmund via Stuttgart, where the 56th Brigade Headquarters of the Pershing Missile Unit was located.

I was at Brigade Headquarters for about three days as my paperwork was processed. From there, Henning and I were picked up by A Battery's mail clerk in his 5/4-ton vehicle, which in essence was a heavy-duty pickup truck. We squeezed into the cab and the ride probably took about two hours on back roads. By the time we arrived at Banderhof, it was dark outside. Harry was assigned to either C Battery or D Battery located at Battalion Headquarters, Neckarsulm Kaserne.

The Army produced a video in 1977 that offers a visual description of the mission of the Pershing Missile Program. The music is a bit dated, but it provides a great overview of the program. It's approximately 10 minutes in length and can be found at the following website:

https://www.youtube.com/watch?v=x7YABPisFGE

Map of Germany – Approximately, the same size as the state of Montana. Heilbronn is in the middle of the map located just north of the city of Stuttgart.

CHAPTER SIX
BADNERHOF KASERNE, HEILBRONN

Finally, we arrived at our new home in Heilbronn at Badnerhof Kaserne (Kaserne is the German word for barracks) where we would be housed primarily for the next two and a half years. I was now a member of Pershing – 7th Army, 56th Brigade, 3rd Battalion 84th Field Artillery Unit, A Battery. To our surprise, as soon as we were shown our room and a bunk, we found out that we would be leaving the next day for our battalion's hot site (CAS – Combat Alert Status) located outside the small town of Kleingartach. We would spend the next twelve weeks living in the secured Administration Building complex. More on Kleingartach later.

Badnerhof were converted WWII German Army barracks and the Kaserne was home to about 500 GIs. We lived in four buildings, two were occupied respectively by Pershing – Batteries A and B, and the other two were occupied by other Army units. We had a mess hall building and a gym. All of these buildings formed a rectangle and in the middle was a huge parade ground for marching, formations, and sports like football, softball, Frisbee, etc.

Badnerhof Kaserne, Heilbronn, Germany. This view is of the parade grounds from the 4th floor. Note: the entrance to the Kaserne is in the middle corner. The gate was guarded by MP's.

There were other buildings on the perimeter. One held the PX, barbershop, laundry, commissary, and movie theatre. There were also various clubs – enlisted men's, NCO's, and Officer's. And there was a chapel used for the various Christian denominations, Jewish, etc. There was a long building that housed the motor pool offices along with many bays for working on trucks, the Engineer Offices and their work area, and other offices used by German Civilians who supported the operations of the complex. Next to that was a huge motor pool lot where both A and B Battery parked their trucks.

Each Battery had 86 vehicles they were responsible for maintaining which included a mixture of jeeps (for officers), (5/4) ton trucks (like a pickup) for general purpose, 2-½ ton trucks (deuce and a half's), and 5-ton trucks, both used for transporting troops or larger items. The inventory of vehicles also included trailers. We also had huge tractors (M757) that pulled the missile trailers and similar vehicles that were the Battery Control Central units (M791) from where the missiles were launched.

These trucks had six-cylinder diesel engines located in the cab between the driver and the passenger. They were so loud that when operating the vehicle, you couldn't carry on a conversation. Another interesting feature about the M757's and M791's was when turning the steering wheel not only do the front wheels turn, but also the two wheels located behind the front wheels – meaning the four front wheels turned. These were the only automatic vehicles that we had, everything else was a stick shift.

All our vehicles were classified as tactical – meaning used for war. The deuce and a halves and the 5-ton trucks had a total of 10 gears forward – a five-speed transmission controlled by using the main stick shift and a two-speed transfer case with a high low lever on the floor. Interestingly, tires on tactical vehicles are designed so that when they leave tread marks on the ground one cannot tell from which direction the vehicle is coming or going. The intake and exhaust pipes of the M757 and M791 were located above the top of the cab and the doors could be pressure sealed at the flip of a switch on the dash. As a result, the entire cab could be immersed underwater allowing for the fording of rivers.

The only other requirement before doing so would be to remove the tension on the fan belt on the motor since there would be too much of a drag on the engine's cooling fan. The deuce and a halves and the five-ton trucks also had raised intake and exhaust pipes allowing them to ford rivers. Below is a photo of an M791 and the vehicle specifications for the M757 and M791.

Canon with the M791 BCC (Battery Control Center) vehicle he drove.

Type: 5-ton 8x8 cargo truck
Manufacturer: Ford
Production: 1968-1969
Assembly: United States
Body and Chassis: M757, M791
Powertrain/ Engine: Continental LDS-465-2 multifuel engine
Length: M757 – 23', M791 – 26'

Heilbronn is located approximately 20 miles north of Stuttgart and I would say it's similar to a large suburban city with a commercial area in the center (but absent the high-rise buildings you find in the U.S.) and a residential section surrounding it. When I was stationed there in the early 1970s, the population was approximately 100,000.

During WWII, there was a nighttime allied bombing mission whose assignment was to destroy a factory in Stuttgart that was producing either aircraft or tanks. Somehow Nazi spies in England got wind of that mission and relayed that information to their superiors in Germany. As a result, Stuttgart went on full blackout and its smaller residential neighbor, the city of Heilbronn, was ordered to keep on its lights. Consequently, Heilbronn was leveled killing many innocent civilians. All that remained after the bombing was the Catholic church and its steeple.

When I speak to various high school students, I share this story, because I believe it's important for them to hear it. To me, the underlying message is that the Nazi War machine was so committed to keeping the war going that they were willing to sacrifice their own citizens to do so.

Another interesting story of Heilbronn involves my neighbor where I lived when I was growing up, William Charles. I used to hang out with his daughters and even had a crush on them when we were young. They moved away when I was 12 and I learned later when I was in Germany that Mr. Charles was in the Army during WWII. He was a captain in the 7th Army, the same Army I was assigned to. During WWII, the 7th Army liberated Heilbronn meaning 25 years before I was stationed there, Mr. Charles helped liberate the same city where I then was assigned permanent duty.

In 2014, there was a movie released titled *The Monuments Men*. It's about a group of allied personnel who were experts in various fine arts such as paintings, sculptures, etc. Their assignment was to locate stolen art that occurred as a result of the Third Reich (I believe millions of pieces of art) and return it to its rightful owner before they were either destroyed or lost forever by those who stole them. I learned from the movie that one of the locations where stolen art was stored was in the salt mines in Heilbronn, Germany.

Residential view of Schwabisch-Gmund, Germany (56th brigade headquarters). Residential Heilbronn was similar.

Remember, when I arrived at Banderhof, I had been trained as a 63B20 (Tactical Fixed Wheeled Vehicle mechanic). I was guaranteed that training when I signed up, however, if you read the fine print I was guaranteed the *training*, not that I would necessarily perform that job once I arrived at my permanent station. As a side note, I took typing in high school. Back then, it was a skill in high demand, and it was even more important in the military. My guess is had they known I possessed that skill I would have been made a clerk typist and spent my tour of duty working in an office. In hindsight, I am glad they didn't know. Being a mechanic in a mobile artillery unit was very challenging at times but was absolutely good for me and I'm proud I served in that role.

Motor Pool April 1972 in front of Admin Bldg at Kleingartach.
Back row: Kidder, Hester, Caldwell, Juan, Kyle, Nixon
Front row: the author, Shorty, Hill, Harrison, Connors
(Not pictured: Peewee, Devon, Holcum, and Summers)

I am honored and proud to have served with these guys and all the others pictured and mentioned throughout this memoir. After returning from 12 weeks at Kleingartach, I was assigned to the big bay room used by other mechanics for living quarters instead of a smaller room because we were low on the totem pole. It was large enough that I bunked with five other guys. One was my friend Henning and four other guys whom I did not know. The only issue I had was that the other guys never wanted to go to bed – even during the week. To resolve this problem, Henning and I negotiated to have our bunks by the windows, then we took all six wall lockers and created a makeshift wall between the two of us and the four other guys. Sleeping was a challenge because they would leave the lights on and play music well into the night. Overall, it was a very unpleasant experience.

Eventually, a two-man room had a vacancy (Donnelson, from Cleveland, OH, was the other occupant) and he invited me to move in with him. I said I could do so only if Henning moved in with us. Donnelson was good with it, so the move was made. Thank God. Donnelson was very easy going, dedicated, and went to bed at a reasonable time. This would remain my primary room for the rest of my tour, though my roommates would change throughout my time there.

Donnelson polishing his shoes in our two-man room.

After Donnelson rotated back home, I invited Krakowski to move in with us. He was a great guy and would become my best friend until he rotated out in March of 1972 which was about a year after we met. An early out program was initiated and many of us qualified. The Army was cutting back because they must have thought they were overstaffed, or it was due to budget cuts. Once you transferred out, you were in the Army Reserves for the remainder of your six-year commitment.

The program must have been very well received because right after Krakowski left, Shorty was next in line from the motor pool for the program. However, the day before he was scheduled to leave, they froze the program. That was a bummer. Back to Krakowski who was from Chicago. He started as Major Kelley's driver but wanted something more (he was a college graduate with a degree in biology from the University of Chicago). So, he was allowed to transfer to the motor pool and became our dispatcher, which involved lots of record-keeping and he loved it.

I have a funny story about Krakowski. Being a biology major in school, he was very much an environmentalist and believed in an organization called Zero Population Growth (ZPG) that professed that no couple should have more than two children to prevent the world from becoming overpopulated. I found his phone number in the mid-nineties after the internet had been developed so, I called him, and we had a nice conversation. He married his sweetheart from college (I don't recall her name, but he missed her a lot when he was in Germany). I asked him how many kids he had, and his answer was eight – yes eight! I asked him about ZPG, and he just laughed. He also became a very successful businessman. His business had something to do with his biology degree.

Now about Shorty. Before joining the Army (he was from Waynesburg, PA), he worked for a tree trimming company during high school. Not long before he enlisted, he was trimming downed branches with a chain saw and it kicked back, and it hit him in the mouth. He lost five teeth and had a fairly prominent scar when I first met him, but it was all but gone by the time he finished his tour. The funny part of the story, if there is one, is he said when he showed his mom after getting home from the emergency room, she nearly fainted.

ON DUTY

Daily life was as follows. We primarily worked five days a week, but from time to time worked weekends as well. Generally, we had the evenings off during the week and we would either hang out in the barracks in someone's room or go to the movies which was our primary form of entertainment. There was a new movie every night and admission cost a quarter.

On the weekends we would often go into town, which I enjoyed. The town was beautiful, and the Germans were friendly. There was a department store called Horten's that felt like a U.S. department store inside, so it reminded me of home.

Horten's department store in downtown Heilbronn.

TRACKING TIME

I probably should have mentioned this earlier, but the military operates on a 24-hour time clock. In other words, they do not use AM or PM. Instead, the day is divided into 24 hours. As an example, 0900 equates to 9AM, 1300 hours equates to 1PM, 1400 hours equates to 2PM, etc. This is a much more efficient way to tell time and I believe most if not all of the rest of the world uses some form of that method.

ORGANIZATIONAL CHART

As a side note, A Battery had five platoons.

- Headquarters platoon – the motor pool was in this platoon and there were about 14 of us (see the photo of us in front of Kleingartach Admin Building later).
- The Commo (communications) platoon.
- Three firing platoons and each one was responsible for three Pershing Missiles.

And our battery had a staff of about 178 soldiers. Also, if you counted all the batteries in the 56th Brigade, there were 108 Pershing Missiles in Germany. Pershing Missiles were two-stage solid propellant missiles measuring 34.4 feet in length (the warhead [WH] was about 39 inches in length), with an externally aimed guidance system. It was designed to deliver nuclear warheads from 110 – 460 miles. As an example, if a missile was fired from St. Louis, MO it could reach the city of Cleveland, OH. They weighed approximately 10,300 pounds and each missile carried one of three warheads – 60 kilotons, 200 kilotons, and 400 kilotons.

The target determined which warhead was used. The 400 kiloton warheads were effectively 30 times more powerful than the two atomic bombs dropped on Japan. However, Pershing Missiles were considered peacekeepers. Meaning, I believe our officers, the President, and Congress never thought they would ever be fired in anger only in retaliation. We were in Germany to keep Russia from doing anything stupid.

Everything associated with the missiles was considered highly top secret at that time. I had a secret security clearance that allowed me to work around the missiles, but I was not authorized to know their capabilities. During the Reagan administration, the missiles were negotiated out of existence as a result of the INF treaty. It took several years to dismantle all the missiles and Russian officials monitored what we did just as we monitored the destruction of their nuclear ground missiles. Interestingly, only two Pershings remain along with two similar Russian missiles, and they are located in pairs – one pair at the Air and Space Museum (in the entrance) in Washington, DC, and the other pair at a museum in Moscow, Russia.

When I speak with high school kids, I start by telling them that the U.S. had a military presence in Europe because of previous conflicts. I tell them I was stationed in Germany during the Cold War, which was a direct result of WWII, which in turn was a direct result of WWI. At the time, there were 250K U.S. military personnel stationed in Germany.

Also, in a book titled *Forty Autumns*, which is an excellent read and one that I would strongly recommend, the author credits the Pershing Missile Program with bringing down the Berlin Wall and ending the Cold War in Europe. It is a true story of a young woman who wanted out of East Germany so badly that she left her entire family behind at very high risk of death and escaped to West Germany. She goes to work for the U.S. government, becomes a U.S. citizen, marries an Army Officer, becomes an Army Officer herself, and is the first female army officer to re-enter East Germany through Checkpoint Charlie to gather information.

SUPERIORS/ COMMANDERS

From time to time, I will mention one or more of the leaders during my tour of duty. I had respect for all of them but liked some more than others. I guess that is typical in any part of a person's life.

BATTERY COMMANDERS

I had two commanders during my 31 months in A Battery: Major Kelley and Captain Spencer, both of whom treated me fairly as well. Of the two, I would say Spencer was more hands-on and mingled with the troops.

TOP

My favorite First Sergeant (Top) was Top McCarthy. He was the last of three Tops there during my tour and he was so good to everyone. One time, he had Shorty, Kidder, and me over to dinner at his house with his family. It was so nice to be in a home-like setting and to have a home-cooked meal. The other two tops were Top McCormack and Top McDonnell who always had a cigar in his mouth. Top McCarthy actually visited me the first summer after I got out. He was driving through St. Louis as his family was relocating to Fort Sill, OK and so we visited for a short time.

Top McCarthy in front of the admin building at Kleingartach.

MOTOR OFFICERS

I recall two motor officers, the first was Lt. White. He was nice, but I don't feel like he ever engaged much with us. Whereas the second motor officer during my tour – Cpt. Donnell – was more actively involved with the motor pool and was very personable. I really liked Cpt. Donnell.

MOTOR SERGEANTS

I had 4 motor sergeants during my tour. All of them were of the rank of either E6 (Staff Sergeant) or E7 (Sergeant First Class). Sergeant Gray was the first and he was good to me. If I had a complaint it was that he allowed me to be transferred to Commo Platoon, which I'll go into later. Sgt. Arcuna was the next. He talked a good game, but he was more talk than action. He left because he was promoted to E8 (Sergeant Major – i.e., Top). Don't get me wrong, I liked him. He brought me back under his line of reporting and for that, I was very grateful. He had been in Vietnam before this assignment. Sergeant David was probably my favorite. He was more personable with a good sense of humor and I feel like I really got to know him. He fully admitted that he was not a mechanic, so always questioned why he was made motor sergeant. I was his subordinate (acting as motor sergeant in his absence). The last arrived just before I got out. His name was Sergeant Kason, and he was not a mechanic. He was nice enough. I just never really got to know him very well, since he was there just a couple of months before I rotated out.

Sergeant Gray – my first motor sergeant.

L to R: Connors, Shorty, Arcuna (motor pool sergeant), and Hill at Kleingartch in the motor pool bays.

L to R: Harrison, Shorty, and David (motor pool sergeant) attacking Shorty at Kleingartach's motor pool lot.

MILITARY DRIVER'S LICENSE

I arrived in Germany in early March and did not obtain a military driver's license until sometime in September. I did drive trucks around the motor pool lot but couldn't leave the Kaserne. Looking back, I was unnecessarily intimidated by the test. It involved learning many European signs – I believe about 200. Many more than you would find in the U.S. manual. As such, we fudged with getting me and another mechanic (Henning) our licenses. They were purchased with a five-gallon can of paint that the tester needed. Yep – it was that easy!

TRANSFER TO COMMO PLATOON

In September of 1971, I was transferred to the communications platoon and I was not happy about it at all. It happened because the commo platoon was the smallest in the battery. The officer and sergeant over that platoon wanted more staff assigned to them (at least that is the story I heard). They negotiated with my motor sergeant to have me reassigned. Fortunately, I was able to negotiate that I still lived with the other motor pool guys but had to stand in formation with the commo platoon. It frustrated me, but they wanted me because they thought I stood out as a mechanic/soldier. During that time, I befriended several guys in the platoon. One of whom was married had a small daughter (about two years old), and they lived off post. Phillip Gallway and his wife Carla – who were both from Wisconsin. I would describe their daughter as what my daughter Jenny was like at that age – this cute little blonde toddler. They very nicely invited me to their apartment around Christmas for dinner in 1971. It gave me a little feeling of home life that Christmas, which helped me a lot. I was very homesick that Christmas. Thanksgiving and Christmas are probably the two most difficult holidays to be in the military so far from home.

Gallway feeding his newborn child.

The first thing I did, when assigned to this platoon, was to perform an inspection of all the vehicles assigned to that platoon. I used a pre-printed vehicle inspection checklist, which was several pages long. It helped me identify all the deficiencies that needed to be corrected. Slowly I made all the necessary repairs, so all their trucks were in good working order. My assignment with that platoon ended about six months later when a new motor sergeant (Arcuna) arrived. He thought I should report to him, so that was that. As I mentioned previously, I was very happy to be re-assigned back to the motor pool.

WORKING ON VEHICLES COULD BE DANGEROUS

Changing tires on the big trucks was dangerous and each truck driver was responsible for changing their tires. There was one time Fontaine, a friend of mine, was changing a tire on his truck (one of the larger ones) and was almost seriously injured. The tire was mounted on a rim and was held in place by a large ring that snapped into place on the outside of the tire. It was not easy to get the ring seated properly and typically you had to beat it into place with a hammer. When airing up one of these tires after being changed you were supposed to have the ringside facing down to the ground. However, my friend mistakenly had it facing up. Because the ring was not properly seated, as the tire pressure increased during inflation, it popped off and struck the guy in the leg. If it had been with more force, it could have broken his leg or worse.

Krakowski and Fontaine in the two-man room where Krakowski and I lived.

During the winter, it was very difficult to work on the trucks, because generally, we worked on them outside. And because the only way to really grip a tool is with your bare hands, we never wore gloves when using tools. As a result, my hands were just freezing in the winter.

BEARING ISSUES WITH THE M757's AND TRAILERS

Once there was an issue with the missile trailers and the M757 tractors that pulled them. The bearings were burning out due to a lack of grease (lubricant). As such, we were directed by brigade command to pull all the wheels and grease the bearings. If you would think this is a very dirty job, you would be correct. There were 12 huge wheels/tires on a tractor and a trailer combined. And each had an inside bearing and an outside bearing.

First, you remove all the lug nuts and pull the tire. You then have to remove the drum which is pressed onto the axle. Then take a brass bar and hammer and tap out each bearing. The brass bar is soft and ensures you do not damage the bearing when tapping it. Then you have to coat the bearing with grease making sure you work it into the individual balls on each bearing. Then reassemble all of it.

It took us several twelve-hour days to complete the assignment. I wore the same uniform each day because it was so messy and at the end, my pants looked and felt like leather there was so much grease caked on them, so I threw away the uniform. My friend Hester thought I was coated with grease including hands and face. In fact, he said the only part of me not covered were my eyes. He also recalls us talking about taking a shower as we walked up the stairs to our barracks late one night. He said I looked at the guys and said, "I'm too tired to take a shower. I think I'll just go to bed." And just smiled at them before heading to the showers.

VEHICLE IDENTIFICATION

Vehicles were marked with several types of stenciling. Typically, in war movies, U.S. military vehicles have a large white star on the hood and the sides of the vehicle or if it is located in a war zone, such as in Vietnam. However, because our vehicles were located in Germany, the stars were painted black. The photo on page 125 is a good example. Also, on the front bumper of vehicles (stenciled in white) was a series of letters and numbers to signify to which unit the vehicle was assigned. The photo on page 160 is a good example. The 7A3F84 stencil on the right side of the bumper indicates 7 Army, 3rd Battalion 84th Field Artillery. On the left side of the bumper, A33 indicates A Battery truck number 33.

OPERATIONAL STATUS AND LACK OF PARTS

We typically had difficulty getting parts for vehicles, but there was one period where several vehicles were not operational because of the lack of parts which was frustrating. So, Shorty and I, working with the motor sergeant at the time (I think Sergeant David), decided to perform a vehicle inspection of all 86 vehicles. This took several days to complete, but it provided a documented report on each vehicle.

All vehicles have some corrections that are needed unless they've just come off the assembly line. However, even many of those deficiencies are considered minor and do not prevent the vehicle from being operational. When the vehicle isn't safe to drive because of these deficiencies it becomes what's called "deadlined" meaning it would be dangerous to operate.

After we finished the inspections it was determined that we had too many deadlined vehicles and as such, the battery was technically out of commission. This got the attention of not only our battery commander (Captain Spencer) but our battalion commander (Lt. Colonel Davis) as well. That meant the battery could not perform its mission and as such that affects not only the battery but the battalion and brigade as well. Pretty quickly we had a meeting with Sergeant David and Captain Donnell to come to a mutual solution to the problem. The solution was that we would not officially file the reports, but also our superiors applied pressure to our supplier to get us some of the critical parts we needed so we could repair enough of our vehicles to allow us to remain an operational battery.

Hill (back to the camera) and Summers removing the towing bar of a broken down 5/4-ton vehicle from our wrecker at Kleingartach. The work the mechanics performed was often dirty and required working with heavy parts, heavy equipment, and heavy tools.

NEW TOOLBOXES

Sometime within my first year in A Battery, several new toolboxes arrived, probably four or five. And just like our uniforms and vehicles, the boxes were painted OD (olive drab) green. I was one of the lucky recipients to receive one and I believe Shorty received one as well. My previous toolbox was incomplete since, for whatever reason, tools disappear over time. It could be the result of carelessly leaving a tool on or under a truck, or someone borrowing a tool and not returning it. Regardless, it becomes more and more difficult to do your job when you don't readily have the tools you need.

So, when I received my new toolbox, complete with 50-60 tools, I was truly excited to have it and was determined to take care of it and not lose any tools. However, over time no matter how hard you try, sometimes a tool gets lost or misplaced. Then you start the process all over again.

KIDDER AND THE LOGBOOKS

When Kidder (from Hornell, NY) took over maintaining the logbooks after Krakowski left on the early out program, the first thing he did was to read all the Army manuals on the subject. As a result, he became an expert in maintaining them. He was so good that when they were inspected by battalion headquarters staff, he was instructing the inspectors on what should be done. He would have received a promotion for it but didn't because of one logbook. This particular book had been at headquarters along with its truck, which had been deadlined for months. Just when it was finally returned to A Battery, the book came with it. Unfortunately, the book had not been maintained while at headquarters and was returned right at the time of another inspection. The book was in bad shape – through no fault of Kidder.

BIRTHDAY CELEBRATION

It was Kidder's birthday and Hester (his roommate) wanted to take him out for a nice dinner. Kidder was sitting on his bed and had started a letter to his mom and dad, which at that point only read – Dear Mom and Dad. While writing he was drinking cherry brandy – probably one of the few drinks he would have. Kidder indicated he wanted to write the letter and suggested to Hester that he go and have a nice meal without him. So, he did, and when he returned about an hour and a half later, Kidder was still working on the letter. However, he hadn't made it very far since it still read Dear Mom and Dad!

ARMY TRAINING

I had been told a long time ago by a good friend who was an Army clerk typist that if the Army knows you can type, they will make you a typist because they were always in high demand. However, Hester's story seems to debunk that myth. He was trained as a mechanic, but never performed those duties. Instead, because he could type, he was immediately made a clerk typist. At least, that's what happened to him while he was stationed in the states.

He eventually and unexpectedly was transferred to Germany. When he arrived at A Battery, he informed our battery commander that he was a clerk typist. The response he received was that according to his records, he had been trained as a mechanic. Hester in turn responded that he had been trained as a mechanic, however, he had never worked as one. He'd only been a typist since he had learned that skill in high school. Our commander's response was, "we don't need typists we need a mechanic; therefore, you will be a mechanic." And that was that!

While Hester was in the motor pool, he was signed up to take a course in low voltage electricity. After he completed the class, he was excited to apply what he had learned. He went to the tool truck to sign out a low voltage regulator and where it should have been located in the tool inventory there was an empty space. When he asked the tool guy (probably Devon) why we didn't have a tester, the reply was that we were not authorized to have one. He then asked the motor sergeant (probably Arcuna) why he was sent to training since we were not authorized to have the tester in the first place and the response was that there was an opening in the class.

INSPECTIONS

Inspections are a way of life in the military as I mentioned earlier. I had them in basic, I had them in AIT, and we also had them in Germany.

We had inspections for our personal area, and these occurred every few months. This means our room, bunk, wall locker, and footlocker. It also included laying out our military gear, such as our ammo belt with ammo pouch, first aid pouch, canteen, harness, mess kit, etc. It all had to be laid out on the floor in a certain order on a blanket folded a certain way. Our two lockers had to have the clothes folded and hung a certain way in a certain place. Our bed had to be made a certain way. Personal effects had to be organized too.

There were inspections to check our areas of daily responsibility. Depending on who it was one group was responsible for the showers and the sinks. Another was responsible for keeping hallways clean, including mopping, waxing, and buffing the floors. The motor pool was responsible for the latrine at our end of the building. Even though we were not assigned the hallways, I did use a buffer from time to time and got pretty good with one. If you don't know how to use one, they will walk you all over the place until you do.

Each morning when we fell in for roll call, we were expected to be dressed in a clean uniform (fatigues), boots polished, and dressed uniformly, such as sleeves up or down, depending upon what command determined was the uniform of the day. We were expected to be clean-shaven (though a mustache was ok), showered, hair within a certain length, etc.

There were inspections for our work area. For the motor pool that meant our office – including the status of all logbooks (one for each vehicle), the bays where we worked on trucks, the inside of the tool truck, the area where trucks were washed. We assisted with ensuring all vehicles were lined up properly (each row in a straight line and ordered by type of vehicle) in the motor pool lot. Also, vehicles were to be clean. Whenever a vehicle returned from being out on maneuvers, or other jobs, the driver was responsible for washing the vehicle at the wash racks.

MUSIC

Music was a big deal in the Army. The guy I roomed with the longest was Shorty (Gacek) and since we both loved our music, we had it going all the time. Most of my LP collection came from when I was in Germany as did almost any of us that loved music. I could buy albums at the PX for $2.50 – double albums were $5. I probably bought about 200 albums while I was there. The most unique album I had was my Woodstock album which I purchased on the German economy, so all the print was in German.

I can recall a few great songs that were released during that time: "Smoke on the Water" by Deep Purple (*Machine Head*), "Oye Como Va" by Santana (*Abraxas*), "We're an American Band" by Grand Funk Railroad (*We're an American Band*), "Take Me Home, Country Roads" by John Denver (*Poems, Prayers and Promises*), "L.A. Woman" by The Doors (*L.A. Woman*), "Iron Man" by White Sabbath (*Paranoid*) and "Easy Livin'" by Uriah Heep (*Demon and Wizards*).

Also, the entire *Who's Next* album by The Who, *Hot Rocks* by the Rolling Stones, *Mark, Don and Mel* by Grand Funk

Railroad, Chicago's *III, IV, and V* albums, the *Woodstock* album, *Tapestry* by Carol King, and the first Crosby, Stills, Nash and Young album – *Deja Vu*. There are many more songs and many other albums that were released during that period, but those are the ones that quickly come to mind. I probably could go on and on.

Each morning, we had formation at about 0730 (pronounced O 7 30) hours after all morning cleaning activities were finished – areas of responsibility and ourselves, and we had finished breakfast. We all had to stand in our respective platoons at parade rest as Top (first sergeant title) gave us important news and our orders for the day. There was a guy (his last name was Williamson) but his nickname was Mad-dog. Anyway, he was a bit of a rebel and was hilarious. Well, there was a great song by Chicago titled "I Just Want to Be Free." Mad-dog's room was on the second floor in the front of the building across from my room. On this particular beautiful spring day, it was sunny and warm. As such, his window was open as were many others. I don't know how he did it, but he had his stereo (turntable or reel to reel tape recorder) timed so that as we stood there in formation the song started to play. It was very loud and echoed off the buildings. Everyone thought it was hilarious except of course Top McDonough (though I bet he was chuckling inside too). He turned from us and looked at the building arms folded and just tapping his foot. The entire battery had a great laugh over that one.

Uriah Heep (a British group) became one of my favorite bands during that time. Interestingly, I learned quite a bit about them after I finished my tour. Ken Hensley (keyboards and vocals) met a TWA stewardess the first time they came to the states to perform. They married and eventually moved to St. Louis. Ken owned a music store in St. Peters, Missouri. At some point, two members of the group David Byron (lead singer) died of liver disease at 38 from alcoholism or drug dependence and Gary Thain (bassist) died at 27 as a result of a heroin overdose.

I learned from some close friends that they attended the same church as Ken – Central Presbyterian in Clayton, MO. Each year he would give a talk from the pulpit about how these two guys died young as a result of alcohol and drugs. Gary had never used heroin before and the first time he did it killed him. He spoke from the heart and targeted the young folks about the dangers of alcoholism and drugs.

Many guys could play instruments, and several brought guitars with them. I believe Hester could play the guitar and drums. Hill was another one that could play the guitar and brought one. I believe he was from North Carolina. I recall he could play well and had a decent voice. Two songs that come to mind that he played were "Rocky Top" and "Tennessee Stud."

M16 ANNUAL RE-QUALIFICATION

Every year we were required to re-qualify with our M16. Remember, first and foremost, all of us were soldiers and if needed would be re-assigned as Infantry. Re-qualifying was a day-long exercise. To get to the rifle ranges (they were not close by), we had to be transported. In this case, it was via a CH47 Chinook Helicopter. I will go into more detail about these amazing helicopters later. At the firing range, we went through the process of firing at targets at a specified distance. We were required to hit a certain number to pass. And before we would do that, we had to ensure they were properly sighted in (accomplished by using a target 25 yards away). I always loved firing my weapon, since I have always enjoyed shooting rifles. And shooting an M16 is nothing short of awesome.

ALCOHOL AND DRUGS

Drugs and alcohol were prevalent and a problem. In the Army in the U.S., you could drink beer at 18. I have several memories to share. First, primarily on the weekends if you walked down the hall you could smell hashish so much that you could probably get high just standing in the hallway. Drinking was so bad that by the end of the weekend the latrine was trashed. Guys would throw up (or worse) all over the place (if you get what I mean). Of course, on the second floor and our half of the hallway, the motor pool guys were responsible for cleaning that latrine. It was a gross responsibility after a weekend.

One of the guys in the motor pool was Hispanic and a great guy. However, after he drank, he would turn into a Hyde kind of guy. You wouldn't want to be around him because he would get very physical and a bit belligerent, and he was as strong as an ox.

Another guy was new to the battery (I never really got to know him), but he got drunk one weekend and was sliding down B Battery's banister when he fell off and broke his neck. My recollection was he had only been with us for a few weeks. It was very sad.

Another guy in the motor pool must have had some psychological problems because several of the times he got drunk he would have contests with other guys where they would place their bare forearms together, then lay a lit cigarette between them. The first one to pull back lost the contest or was considered a chicken. Needless to say, he had burn marks all over his arms. I found it a bit bizarre.

I heard once when we were on status at Kleingartch, an officer walked in on a bunch of guys smoking hashish (which I was told was much stronger than marijuana) and turned around and walked out. It was that prevalent and for some officers, it was just easier to look the other way than to place guys on report.

Some guys used toothpaste tubes to ship drugs home because they believed the smell of the drugs could not be detected that way.

Mad-dog shipped a motorcycle home by dismantling it and sent it piece by piece. He also used it as an opportunity to ship drugs home in the hollow frame of the cycle.

From time to time, we had to vacate our building so the MP's could go through the building and our personal effects to see if anyone was hiding drugs.

MURDER

Another tragic death that took place in our battalion was a murder. There was a guy in A Battery (Gannon), pictured below, who was eventually transferred to battalion headquarters at Neckarsulm. He lived on the fourth floor of his barracks, and the way the story goes is that he was dealing drugs and angered someone who later stabbed him while he was sleeping. For whatever reason, at one point I was at battalion headquarters and someone showed me the bed that he was supposedly stabbed in.

L to R: Canon, Henning, Krakowski, and Gannon.

ALCOHOL, DRUGS, AND ME PERSONALLY

I didn't do drugs as it was a matter of principle for me. A couple of my friends were the same way however, I had other good friends who chose to partake. In retrospect, I believe the reason I never succumbed to the pressure to use them (and there was pressure), was because I realized I didn't like being out of control. And it seemed to me that when you use drugs your mind is not what it normally would be, and you lose control of yourself.

Because I came from an alcoholic family (my father), I hated alcohol for the most part. I did drink but didn't really start until I got to Germany. I only drank hard liquor once and truly did not like it and regretted it. About four months after getting to Germany one of my so-called motor pool friends (the one with the cigarette burns), took me to a Gasthaus in town and started buying drinks. Well, he had me drunk before I knew it. In fact, I left pretty quickly (I think I took a bus) back to the Kaserne.

All I remember was collapsing on the bunk, then leaning over and vomiting all over the floor. However, because I hated cleaning up after guys in the latrine, I had the presence of mind to get up, clean up my mess, and then collapse back onto my bunk. I don't think I woke up until the next day and when I did, I had a terrific hangover. I will admit to getting slightly drunk two other times. Once, was when we were on status at Kleingartach. I had had several beers and for whatever reason, a bunch of guys decided to play football. I went to play too, and at first, could not figure out why I was unable to catch a pass that went right through my hands.

The other time was during Octoberfest when we went to the carnival in town. One-liter steins of beer were served in the beer tents and after one of those, I was pretty light-headed. Then someone got the brilliant idea to take a ride on the western roundup, a huge circular cage that goes around and then tilts up at an angle with the ground. I felt lousy after riding that thing. If you can picture the scene in *The Sandlot* of the guys chewing tobacco and then getting on a ride, you would have a good indication of how I felt. So even though I did overindulge a few times, that was it.

In the Army, most guys smoked, but not all. I smoked before I went in and continued while in the Army. We were allotted four cartons a month and a carton cost $2.50 so smoking was a very inexpensive habit. I smoked about 2 ½ packs a day, however, most of those would burn up because I might be working on a truck and needed to set the cigarette aside. I knew I wanted to quit after returning home, I just needed a reason. Well, that reason was Janet Murphy (Heyer). Within four months of meeting her, she convinced me to quit and I did so – cold turkey.

PROMOTIONS

I received several promotions while serving. I started in Basic Training as an E1. I did not make E2 until I finished AIT, which was early March of 1971. That meant I now had one stripe (chevron) on my uniform. Shortly, after arriving at my assignment of A Battery, I was promoted to E3, which was one stripe and a rocker stripe underneath (private first class). By September I was promoted to E4 (called Spec 4) or Specialist. I received my Sergeants Rank (E5) in March/April of 1972 – that's three stripes on my sleeve. Major Kelley was the Commanding Officer who ensured I was promoted to sergeant (not Spec 5). That would be my rank for the remainder of my service. I was proud of achieving that rank at the age of 20.

PATCHES, MEDALS, AND OTHER AWARDS

The patch I wore on my left sleeve for the first year I was in Germany was the 7th Army patch. It was called 7 Steps to Hell because there were 7 steps on the patch. After about a year (I believe May 1972), the 56th Brigade was awarded a special patch that we then switched to. It had the Pershing Missile on it with lightning on either side of the missile. We were still within the 7th Army, we just now had a more specialized identification. We wore these patches on our left sleeve. If I remember correctly, you wore the patch on your right sleeve if you were serving in a combat zone.

7th Army   Pershing Missile Brigade

Another change to our uniform that the brigade headquarters attempted but were unsuccessful in was to have our dress uniform hat changed to a beret. I believe they were trying for a maroon color. As an example, the green berets obviously had a beret that was OD green.

I also earned several medals. Several of these were received by anyone who served at the same time, one of which was the National Defense Ribbon:

> The National Defense Service Medal (NDSM) is a service award of the United States Armed Forces established by President Dwight D. Eisenhower in 1953. It is awarded to every member of the US Armed Forces who have served during any one of four specified periods of armed conflict or national emergency from 1950 to the present. Combat or "in theater" service is not a requirement for the award.

I also received the Sharpshooter Medal for having hit more than 80 but less than 91 targets during my required basic training firing tests. A Marksman Medal required hitting between 71 and 80 targets. An Expert Medal required hitting 91 or more targets. I would have earned that medal but missed too many hits the night we were at the night range in basic.

> A sharpshooter is one who is highly proficient at firing firearms or other projectile weapons accurately. Military units composed of sharpshooters were important factors in 19th-century combat. Along with "marksman" and "expert", "sharpshooter" is one of the three marksmanship badges awarded by the U.S. Army.

Because my battalion acted heroically during WWII on two separate occasions, I was authorized to wear a citation with one oak leaf cluster. However, I've never been able to determine how they were earned. While I was assigned to the commo platoon, I was put in for what was called the Pershing Pickle, so-called because it was in the shape of a pickle. I was awarded that badge because my superiors thought I was doing a job that exemplified the motto of the unit – QRA (Quick, Reliable, and Accurate).

> The Pershing Professionals Badge is a local individual award created by the 56th Artillery Group to recognize proficiency on the nuclear Pershing missile system. It was awarded from December 1968 through 1979.

On my certificate it states the following: "In recognition of outstanding achievement, QUICK, RELIABLE, ACCURATE performance and devotion to duty while assigned as a member of this command. He has established himself as truly deserving of this coveted award and has exhibited the proper traits of a PERSHING PROFESSIONAL, TO WIT: For outstanding performance of the duties of vehicle mechanic in the communications platoon of a Pershing Missile Firing Battery. His high degree of dependability and continuing devotion to duty has led to the improvement of overall vehicle maintenance in the communications platoon. Specialist Heyer's pride in his accomplishments and his "can do" attitude have proved to be an asset to the battery as well as this platoon. His consistent attention to detail and constant professional attitude are indeed deserving of this recognition."

The last medal I received was my Good Conduct Medal.

> The criteria for a Good Conduct Medal are defined by Executive Orders 8809, 9323, and 10444. The Good Conduct Medal, each one specific to one of the five branches of the U.S. Armed Forces, is currently awarded to any active duty enlisted member of the United States military who completes three consecutive years of "honorable and faithful service". Such service implies that a standard enlistment was completed without any non-judicial punishment, disciplinary infractions, or court martial offenses.

Near the end of my tour, all officers and NCO's—including Shorty and myself—were called into a meeting by our Commander Captain Spencer. During that meeting, the captain told all in attendance that he wanted more awards to be given to the staff. He specifically stated that he thought Shorty and I should be put in for the Army Commendation Medal, but for whatever reason, it didn't happen. I would have loved to have received that medal as it is given to those that performed an exceptional job while serving. Still, it made me feel very good that the captain believed Shorty and I had earned that recognition.

> The Army Commendation Medal is awarded to any member of the Armed Forces of the United

States other than General Officers who, while serving in any capacity with the U.S. Army after December 6, 1941, distinguished themselves by heroism, meritorious achievement or meritorious service.

CQ DUTY

The office is always staffed – even overnight and on weekends. CQ Duty exists after normal business hours. I had it once or twice and it made for a very long night. I don't recall having to do much – mostly just be available and monitor activity. One of the duties as CQ is to go to each room at 0500 – 0530 hours to wake everyone. That was not my favorite task.

Once another sergeant—a lifer (career soldier)--was pulling CQ Duty and he came into the room I shared with Shorty, turned on the lights, and said loudly that it was time to get up. My bunk was closest to the door. By this time, I was also a sergeant, but I was an E5 Sergeant, and he was an E6 Staff Sergeant. Now, I'm a morning person but still didn't seem to move quickly enough for this guy. And when he kicked one of the corners of my bed, I told him to f*** off. I didn't even realize I had said it. So, when I heard he was going to write me up and put me on report, I was very upset. Fortunately, nothing ever came of it.

MANEUVERS

I mention maneuvers many times throughout this memoir because of how often they occurred. I recollect that we went on maneuvers several times during my tour (maybe once per year). A couple of maneuvers were during pleasant weather and were not too bad. Generally, during such outings, the motor pool didn't have much to do, so often we would be assigned guard duty. Interestingly, many of these outings were on private property (woods owned by various farmers or other German landowners). Most of the time, we would tear up the woods and neighboring fields because of the large, heavy trucks we used. I don't know if it's accurate, but I once heard that this destruction would cost the Army tens of thousands of dollars (marks) that would have to be reimbursed to the owner. For reference, at that time you could get about four marks to the dollar which made German goods and food very cheap for us.

The most challenging outing we had was in the middle of winter. We stayed out for five days and it was cold and snowy. I only recall a few tidbits about this trip, but they were memorable. It was the first (and only) time I had to relieve myself outside in the cold and we did not bathe or shave for the duration. We all looked terrible by the time it was over. It was very difficult to find a warm place to sleep and I remember at least one or two of the nights sleeping in the mess tent on the ground in our sleeping bags in front of a 1,000 BTU heater that was loud and the forced air felt like a wind tunnel. It ran on diesel fuel so it was loud and would drown out most conversations in the very large tent.

On maneuvers, in the field during winter.

EUROPE ON RED ALERT

In the spring of 1972, President Nixon decided to place mines in the harbor of Haiphong, Vietnam. This was one of the main ports for North Vietnam to receive supplies from those countries that supported their cause (primarily China). The U.S. public was unaware that because of that act, all of NATO military forces in Europe went on high alert (DEFCON 3?). As a result, all Officers and NCO's (i.e., sergeants - non-commissioned officers) were called into a meeting. And since I had just made the rank of sergeant (E5), I was part of that meeting at just 20 years old.

We were informed that we were on high alert and as a result, we would probably go to war with Russia, China, or both. The belief was that we would be awakened sometime that night and be issued our M16's with live rounds of ammo. Mechanics would be issued incendiary grenades for deadlined trucks. These grenades are placed by the engine block because they're phosphorus and get so hot they melt the block of the engine therefore making it useless for the enemy. We would then go to the field and launch our missiles at pre-determined targets. Our commanding officer shared that Russia would in turn launch its missiles. I learned later that should our missiles be fired we had an estimated seven minutes to live. Because the Russians would have detected our launch and in turn launched their missiles at us. Needless to say, I was scared as hell. I thought that if that occurred the world would end as we know it and that I would never see my family again. Fortunately, sanity prevailed, and nothing happened. We may have been at odds with Russia, but they didn't want a nuclear war any more than we did.

LEAVE

In the military, you get 30 days off per year. I only took one 30-day leave in Germany and it was halfway through my tour of 31 months at the end of May 1972. The day I left St. Louis to return to Germany I said goodbye to my family at Lambert airport. I was doing okay until I hugged my mom goodbye and saw my little brother Steve, who was 12 at the time, crying. I lost it after that. I remember being at the Frankfurt train station waiting to catch a train and was very sad. However, when I got to the Kaserne and had to walk across the parade grounds towards my barracks, I was as sad as I had ever been. I knew I now had another 15 months before I could go home for good. It was a tough time for me, and I got very depressed.

The day before I was to return from leave is easy for me to recall. It was on June 23, 1972. That evening a plane had been hijacked and was parked on the tarmac at Lambert St. Louis International Airport. While the plane was sitting on the tarmac and Federal authorities were negotiating with the hijacker, someone drove their car through the perimeter fence and rammed the landing gear on the plane at 80 mph, thus making it inoperable.

ARTICLE 15

As a sergeant, I was responsible for giving out assignments to the motor pool mechanics. One time we were a bit slow, so my boss Sergeant Arcuna, wanted the truck bays cleaned because the floors were going to be painted gray, which meant that all the grease and dirt had to be removed from the floor. It was not easy to remove the grease. Everyone was working on it just fine except one guy who was new to the group. He refused to help.

I asked him several times to help the others, but he just stood there. I think he was testing my authority because I had not been a sergeant very long. Finally, I told him that I did not want to do this but that I was giving him a direct order to help. When that didn't work, I told him I was going to put him on report. I went to Arcuna and did so. The guy was given an Article 15, which goes on your record and it has a monetary fine associated with it. He was also transferred out right away because he was considered a troublemaker.

View of A Battery motor pool lot containing 86 vehicles.

A NEW SHIPMENT OF HEATERS

This is probably not a well-known fact, but almost all our trucks in Germany didn't have heaters in them. I believe the only ones that did were the newer trucks we received. Similar to parts of the U.S., Germany gets very cold in winter! We once received a shipment of heaters--maybe a dozen or so–and we became the most popular guys in the world. The heater kits consisted of the heater that was mounted under the dashboard on the passenger side, two hoses that connected to the cooling system of the engine (to the engine block), and a thermostat that regulated the water temperature.

First, we took care of our own vehicles. The motor pool had four trucks including our motor officer's jeep, so we installed heaters in each of those and we ensured our commanding officer received one as well. Other than that, it was wide open. Guys were trying to bribe us so we would install one in their trucks. I don't recall how they were divided up, but they were all gone pretty quickly.

PEEWEE

One of the guys with whom I served was nicknamed Peewee. Can you guess why? He was about 10 years older than the rest of us, a lifer, and a Spec 5 (Specialist), probably because he didn't want supervisory responsibility. He was a nice guy and a good mechanic, and he was a fuel truck driver in Vietnam before being assigned to A Battery in Germany. One story he told was that Vietnamese children were taught how to take a live grenade, unscrew the gas cap on a truck, drop the grenade in the tank, replace the cap, then walk away. The resulting explosion if it was a fuel truck would be catastrophic. But the Vietnamese were a very superstitious people so Peewee welded two poles – one to each side of his front bumper – and on top of each, he placed a human skull to keep the kids away from his truck. His commander got wind of this and made him remove the human skulls. Instead, he placed cow skulls on the poles and that worked just as well.

I have another story about Peewee that conveys his sense of humor. Truck drivers were responsible for performing simple maintenance on their vehicles such as changing tires, changing the oil, etc. There was a young guy who was new to the battery and we learned rather quickly that he had no clue how to change the oil in his truck or perform any other type of standard vehicle maintenance.

Sometime in the spring, Peewee was explaining to this guy that he needed to drain the winter air out of his tires and replace it with summer air. I don't know how Peewee kept a straight face, but the guy was trying to understand how he was going to follow these instructions. Needless to say, eventually the guy figured out that Peewee was just teasing him.

However, this guy also did something that was not too smart. We found out that he drained the oil from his truck, but when he refilled it he added so much oil that it was spilling out of the filing hole at the top of the valve cover on the top of the engine. It was probably three times the amount of oil that should have been added.

I'm not sure he would have been able to start his truck, but I have to believe that if he had done so, it would have blown every seal out of the engine. If it wouldn't have ruined the motor, it most certainly would have needed to be completely disassembled and every engine seal replaced. That would have been a huge job that would not have performed by us. Instead, it would have been necessary to transfer it to Service Battery located at Battalion Headquarters Neckarsulm Kaserne.

There were times we had a problem with a vehicle and would try to figure out the problem. As an example, a bolt was stripped so we were unable to remove it. Peewee would then say, "We just gotta get smarter than the bolt."

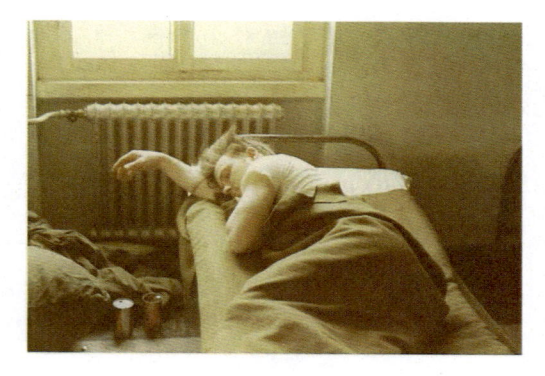

Peewee sleeping in at Kleingartach. He lived off post with his wife, so he only slept there if we had a late night of work.

MOTOR POOL BUDDIES AND OTHERS

I made friends with a number of guys while I was in. Most were in the motor pool and they are named throughout this memoir. However, I made several other friends from within the battery. There were three guys in the office: Belt (from New Hamshire), Henneman (the Bronx), and Squirrel (don't recall his real name, but he was from West Virginia and loved the song "Take Me Home Country Roads" by John Denver).

He loved to take naps during the day and since he lived on the first floor in the back of the building, he was easily able to pull it off. He would leave his window unlocked and had a barrel outside his window. After lunch, he would sneak around the back and climb through his window and take a nap. No one knew he was in there because his door was locked from the outside making it appear as though the room was empty.

Belt got me hooked on enjoying a glazed donut with my coffee during our morning break. We would cut up the donut and dip it in our coffee and of course, it made our coffee taste much sweeter. Griffon was a cook and a good friend. In fact, I was good friends with all the cooks. There was a guy by the name of Canon who was from Texas and drove the BCC (Battery Control Center vehicle - M791). One of the funniest statements he would often make was, "if you throw enough mud up against the wall, sooner or later some of it's going to stick." Another statement he would often make was, "just like downtown." This was in reference to a place or a thing.

In downtown Heilbronn.
Front row: Belt and Squirrel. Back row: Krakowski and Canon.

Another guy in the motor pool was Jones (he managed the tool truck and was our purchasing agent). Two funny things about him. First, he slept with his eyes open which was very weird. Second, he used to make a fish face. It was very funny. Anytime we went to the movies, we would try to bribe him to go up on the stage and make his face. We all offered him $5 each, but he never took us up on it.

Jones who ran the tool truck and was our purchasing agent.

There were a couple of guys from Commo Platoon and both happened to be from Missouri, but I do not recall their names. Another guy in the Commo Platoon (Schwartz) used to love to give heart punches. Essentially, it was a punch to the chest, and it used to really tick me off when he did it. I finally got angry enough about it and yelled at him to stop doing it and he stopped.

There was another guy who went by the name Mighty Fine. I found it amusing that he went by that name. He was a good guy from what I recall. I believe he rotated out within a year of my getting there.

Mighty Fine in our room at Badnerhof Kaserne.

Because Babich (one of my best friends) was the mail clerk, he was exempt from all other duties such as guard duty, KP, attending reveille (morning formation), etc. Before he became the mail clerk, however, he was a commander's driver. It was almost like he was the officers' personal valet. He had to drop off and pick up his laundry, keep his jeep polished (remember it was a tactical vehicle, so it should be flat, not shiny so it blends in with its surroundings in the woods), etc.

And finally, I knew several guys from Engineering. These were the guys that kept all the generators operational – and we had a lot of generators. The craziest of them was Mad-dog Williamson who I already mentioned previously.

SURPRISE PRACTICE ALERT

One day while at the motor pool, we heard rumors there was going to be a surprise alert. I believe it was a Friday and all of us were grumbling about it. Again, by that time Shorty and I were both sergeants. Well no sooner had we walked into our room in our barracks than the alarm went off. Shorty and I flew down the stairs, ran across the parade ground and down towards the commissary. We hid out for a while and ate dinner there.

About an hour later we returned to the barracks and *everyone* was gone. Everyone had to go to a nearby training site called Redleg about a 15-minute drive away. Anyway, Shorty and I hung out in our room for a while and finally realized we had made a huge mistake. Technically, we were AWOL (absent without leave) and that could get you into serious trouble. We somehow managed to hitch a ride up to Redleg and when we found the building where the motor pool guys were located, we discovered our motor officer was there as well. We made some lame excuses that we had left the post and were out when the alarm sounded. It was a line of bull. He looked at us suspiciously but let us off the hook. Thank God.

NEW JEEPS

One time we received a shipment of new jeeps – maybe six – and to retrieve them several of the motor pool guys drove to a rail yard located in Ludwigsburg. It was just outside of Stuttgart, located between Heilbronn and Stuttgart. It was so cool to get to drive them right off the flat cars on which they were shipped and then back to Badnerhof.

FOOD RUNS

There was a small Gasthaus (Tilley's) just outside of the Kaserne. Every so often someone would notify us that they were making a food run there and ask if anybody wanted anything. Their food was great, and it wasn't Army food. The standard agreement was, "if you buy, I will fly." They had what was called a liver-case sandwich and it was amazing. It came with some potato salad and was a great treat. You could also get a ham and swiss cheese sandwich. There was an old German guy who either worked there or hung out there a lot. It seems like anytime I was in there, so was he. He knew a couple of English words but really liked to say s**t and g********t. That's all he knew, and he would always say them together. It was hilarious.

ENLISTED MEN'S CLUB OR NCO CLUB

If you wanted a good steak, you could go to the enlisted men's club, or if you were an NCO (non-commissioned officer) you would go to the NCO club. Either way, it was the best way to get a steak dinner, which again was not Army food.

BORROWING MONEY FROM GUYS

I have one personal instance where Spec 5 Crown borrowed some money from me, and I had a very tough time getting him to pay me back. He always seemed to conveniently be broke anytime I approached him. Finally, I realized the best time to ask him was on payday right after he received his money. He was still hesitant but did finally pay me. I believe this was not more than a couple of months before he was killed, which I cover later in this memoir.

CALLING HOME

I only called home once maybe twice during my tour because it was so expensive. You had to go into downtown Heilbronn to the Bundespost (post office), hand someone behind the counter the number for your call, and let them know it was in the U.S. You then waited as they placed the call. Once the connection was made, you entered a booth and picked up the phone. My recollection is a half-hour call cost approximately $60. When you make only a few hundred dollars a month, that was a lot of money.

MAIL CALL

Mail call was exactly as you would picture it. As we got off work about 1700 hours, the mail clerk would have mail ready for us. He would stand just outside the mailroom and begin calling out the names of those who had mail that day. You would stand there and wait to hear your name called.

Mail was typically how we communicated with our friends and family back home. I primarily wrote my family, though on one or two occasions I wrote my Grandpa and Grandma McGee. I also wrote to my brothers Rick and Steve a few times and my friends Dave and Jane. I think I wrote Buzz and Leroy once – two mechanics at Tom's gas station where I worked before entering the Army. I wrote to my ex-girlfriend Donna early on and then later another ex-girlfriend Sally whom I dated briefly before the Army and then briefly after I first got out. The bottom line is that we knew if we wanted to receive mail, we needed to write home and send letters to others. I seem to recall I wrote to my parents weekly. I also took lots of photographs and sent them home.

Conversely, my mom was taking lots of photos of home life and sending them to me. I very much appreciated her doing that as it made me feel like I had a connection to my family and home.

The first time I wrote home from Germany was at Kleingartach because we moved there the day after I arrived at A Battery. I wrote letters to about seven relatives and friends letting them know I got to Germany. However, I did not have stamps and incorrectly thought that I could mail them without stamps and that the postal worker would collect the cost of a stamp when he or she delivered the letter. Obviously, I was very wrong.

All the letters came back the next day. The mail clerk handed all of them back to me during mail call. Because there were so many being returned, he saw that many of them were sent to a Kirkwood, Missouri address. He then informed me that he went to the University of Wisconsin with a guy from Kirkwood. He asked if I knew the last name Colton. Ironically, it was a good Catholic family with many kids (10 I believe) that attended the same Parish and school as me. My answer was, of course, I knew them. The other interesting aspect of this was that family lived caddy-corner to where my future wife Janet lived whom I had not met yet.

During my tour, there were four mail clerks. The first was the guy I mentioned above. The next guy's name was Waldon. I remember him as a very nice, soft-spoken easygoing guy. After he left, Babich arrived and would become one of my closest friends and we remain close to this day. Babich was from Livonia, MI. After Babich left, which was not long before I did (about two months), there was another mail clerk whom I never really got to know.

Waldon – the second mail clerk for A Battery.

TELEVISION

There was no television for most of my tour. In my last year, workers began to build a new tower near our building, and it was probably about 200 feet high. The result was we now had cable tv but I never really watched it. The only television in the building was located in the Day Room, where there was also a pool table, foosball table, a ping pong table, and a small library. Going to the movies (almost nightly) took its place.

STARS AND STRIPES

Our only access to news was to read the newspaper. The military newspaper is called *Stars and Stripes* and was founded on November 9, 1861, during the Civil War. I would often obtain a copy, so I could stay current with what was going on in the U.S. and the world. Occasionally, my parents would send me a copy of the *St. Louis Globe-Democrat* – the local newspaper they subscribed to. I would enjoy reading it since it gave me a feeling of being connected to my hometown.

SNACK SHACK

I never understood this, but there was a small shack located near our building where a German lady who was rather well-endowed sold snacks such as hot dogs, chips, etc. It just seemed out of place.

3 COIN

Babich, Shorty, and I had a game we played all the time called 3 coin. The rules were that we would all flip a coin until two of us had either heads or tails and the third guy had the opposite resulting in losing the flip. Whoever lost had to pay for whatever we were planning to do – go to the movies, go out to eat, etc.

MISSILE LAUNCH

Once a year a battery was selected to take three of their missiles to the U.S. (Cape Canaveral in this instance) and launch them which was a very big deal. The firing platoon guys practiced all the time, however, there is nothing like actually participating in a launch. I guess because I had been doing a good job, I was approached in February of 1973 to see if I would like to go on one of the trips. I declined and recommended that Hester go in my place because he lived in Georgia and would have time to see his future wife, Linda, (whom he got engaged to during that trip).

As a sergeant though, I did participate in the convoy that transported three of our missiles and all other necessary support vehicles to Ramstein Airbase where they were loaded into massive cargo planes where the nose opens on the plane. I assume they were C-5 Galaxies and remember how massive they were. As an example, we were able to park four missiles each on their respective trailer inside one of those planes in a configuration that consisted of two deep and two side by side. There were only inches to spare on all sides, but we got it done. It was amazing to see these huge missiles on trailers parked inside. A photo and the specifications of the C5 Galaxy are below.

C5 Galaxy Specs:
Length: 247 feet, 10 inches (75.3 meters)
Height at Tail: 65 feet, 1 inch (19.8 meters)
Max Takeoff Weight: 769,000 pounds (346,000 kilograms)

SALTY LANGUAGE

One of the things you'd notice on a military base is the language where every other word is f***. I can only recall two guys (Hester and Kidder) who never used foul language. However, they never seemed to be bothered by those of us who did. I will say that as soon as I returned home, I was able to turn off that vocabulary so that I might only use it when I was with other guys.

GERMAN LANGUAGE

I'm often asked if I learned German while living in that country and I always explain that I learned a few phrases, but because I lived on an Army Base, there really wasn't the opportunity to learn and practice the language. However, just before Shorty and I started on a new program (working in the German economy which I cover later) designed to assist us with rotating out of the Army, we took a basic German class that was now being used for new arrivals. The lady who taught the class was an older German who was a child during WWII.

She is the one who shared the story of Heilbronn with us. She indicated Germans were not upset with the Allied Forces fighting the German Army, destroying a good part of their country, and ending the war. They accepted full responsibility for putting Hitler in office and allowing him to become a dictator and ultimately ruining their country and starting WWII.

GERMAN WEATHER

The average temperature in Germany during the 1970s was moderate. In winter, the temperature was generally in the low 30's. In the summertime, the temperature was generally in the low 70's. For the most part, it was quite comfortable. Obviously, there were extremes from time to time.

As an example, in the winter if the wind was blowing strongly it could be very cold and uncomfortable to be outside. During spring and fall, we would sleep with our window open and it was quite nice. Interestingly, we did not have screens on our windows because there are no mosquitos or other flying insects in Germany. Since our barracks only had heat in the winter (radiator), but no air conditioning, we would often sleep with our windows open in the summer as well.

MERCEDES 230 SL CONVERTIBLE

The summer before I got out in 1973, my motor officer (Captain Donnell) had a Mercedes convertible sports car. At one point he went back to the states on leave, during which time, he let Shorty and me have use of his car. Now Shorty was the only one of us who had a civilian license, but we tooled around everywhere in that car with him behind the wheel and me in the passenger seat. It was August and Grand Funk Railroad's song "We're an American Band" was all over the Armed Forces Network Radio Station. We could not have had it better. Getting out soon (Shorty in September and me in October) and having a cool sports car to drive around was awesome. We did, however, have one mishap.

Shorty was down by the truck washing pits in front of the motor pool offices and decided he wanted to burn rubber and see how quickly he could get the car moving so he floored it – the car was a stick shift. Well in attempting to do so, he blew out the rear end of the car. All we could think was the captain is going to kill us. So, we pushed it into a bay and tried to repair it ourselves.

The only problem was our tools were in inches and the car was metric. Eventually, we had to have it towed to the dealer, then tell Captain Donnell what had happened after he returned. Fortunately, the mechanic at the dealer indicated the parts were defective and thus it was not our fault. They were going to fail soon anyway. God, we were lucky! Either way, Captain Donnell didn't seem to be bothered by the whole incident.

CAPTAIN SPENCER

Captain Spencer was the second commanding officer of our Battery while I was there and for some reason, he really liked me. One time late in my tour, I was working on an old five-ton transport truck. By then I was a sergeant and typically sergeants didn't work on trucks but rather assigned the work to the enlisted men. I was running a new wiring harness (the entire harness was one piece and ran to all the various electrical connections). I was having a blast, pulling out the old and replacing it with the new one. I was on my back up under the dashboard of the truck when I heard the captain announce himself. I climbed out and we chatted briefly, and he started to walk away as I climbed back under the dash. In a moment of frustration, I said, "Jesus Christ!" About 10 seconds later the captain returned and said, "Did you call me Sergeant Heyer?" Needless to say, he was hilarious and we both had a good laugh.

When it came time for the captain to have his Volvo inspected by the Germans so he could drive it, he went to Hester and asked what was needed for it to pass. The payment required so that you could avoid an actual inspection with a POV (privately owned vehicle) was 1/5 of liquor and a carton of cigarettes. Hester made all the arrangements and worked out the exchange of goods and services, and ultimately took care of it for the captain.

For some reason, someone in the motor pool (Kidder and Shorty for their race car 61) had a VW Bug engine on the floor of the office. The captain happened to be touring the area and noticed it on the floor and asked, "what is that?" Kidder or Hester replied that it was a VW engine. The captain stated that it was from a POV and thus unauthorized to be in the office. He wanted it removed by end of the day.

It happened to be late by the time Kidder and Hester realized it hadn't been moved, but they were tired and decided to move it the next day. The following morning, they were walking in the dark heading to the motor pool (don't know where the rest of us were – maybe trailing behind) when they noticed someone standing by the motor pool office door waiting to get in. Kidder and Hester thought it was a driver wanting to check out a truck. Nope - it was the captain.

He wanted to see if the motor had been moved as he had ordered. One of the guys made the excuse that the day got away from them and so they planned to move it that morning. The captain's reply was, "did you sleep last night?" Obviously, they replied, "yes sir." He then said, "then you did have time to move it." That is what I liked so much about the captain. He was no-nonsense but had a great sense of humor. I believe he had a soft spot for the motor pool guys because he knew how critical we were to the operations of the mission since we were mobile artillery.

Kidder posing with two VW bug engines on the floor of the motor pool office. One of which is the engine that got him and Shorty in trouble with Spencer.

5/4 TON ACCIDENT

About a month or two before I rotated back to the states, I was involved in a car accident with a Mercedes Benz. I was driving back from Redleg to Badnerhoff Kaserne when I came upon a broken down A Battery truck, so I stopped to help the guy. I quickly realized I would need to run to the motor pool to obtain a part and return to the truck so I could complete the repair. I climbed into A61, the motor pool's 5/4-ton vehicle I was driving and pulled out onto the road. At that moment, a Mercedes was going by in the same direction. He veered off the road and hit the side of a garage. The car and the garage were damaged, so the MP's were called in as well as the Bundespolizei (German Police). I was terrified that I would be detained and thus unable to go home when my tour was over. The entire investigation was based on one piece of evidence: did I have my turn signal on when I pulled onto the road and into traffic. I said I did, and I believe the German citizen insisted I did not. He was going rather fast – probably faster than he should have been. However, in all honesty, to this day I do not recall if I used my turn signal or not. Because it was his word against mine, the investigation was closed.

1972 OLYMPICS

During the summer Olympics in Munich, there were random drawings for tickets so GI's (Government Issue) could attend one of the events and I won a ticket to some bike races. Again, being the homebody that I was, I gave my ticket to Connors. Tragically, during the two/three-week period several Israeli

Athletes were murdered by Muslim Terrorists. To this day the incident is still a cloud that hangs over those games.

On his way to the Olympics, Connors was able to visit the Dachau Concentration camp, which is located just outside of Munich. He told me later that it was a very sobering experience visiting the site where so many innocent victims, primarily Jewish families, were murdered and the fact that this location along with all the other concentration camps located in Germany and Poland, was an organized and concerted effort by the Nazis to exterminate the Jewish population in Europe. The thought of that makes me sick to this day.

A GHOST STORY

Connors was from Buffalo, New York and he once shared a story about his house being haunted and some of the weird things that occurred. There was a couple who lived there, and the husband had hung a chandelier for his wife in the dining room but must not have mounted it properly. Eventually, it fell and killed his wife. The husband was so distraught over her death that he hung himself in the garage and was supposedly the spirit that lived in the house.

Connors gave examples of some of the odd occurrences, one being that his dog would bark anytime the spirit entered the room. The house also had a staircase that went to the second story. And Connors's parents changed the configuration from straight to a 90-degree angle with a landing in the middle. At night, the ghost would walk down the stairs (you could hear the footsteps according to Connors) and because the stairway configuration had changed, the ghost would run into the railing, then change course and finish walking down the stairs.

Connors also roomed with me for a while. When he arrived at A Battery, he had a girlfriend from the states, Katie, that he was crazy about. Not too long after Connors arrived, she broke up with him. He took it very hard, which I believe anyone under the same circumstances would have. After that, he got a bit wild. He stayed out late at night and eventually met a German girl. He moved in with her and I believe they eventually married (after I left) and still are to this day.

CHAPTER SEVEN
KLEINGARTACH, GERMANY CAS (COMBAT ALERT SITE)

Convoy lined up at Redleg preparing to relocate to Kleingartach (CAS) site. Notice the tarps draped over the missiles.

Kleingartach is about 15 miles west of Heilbronn and the CAS site there was where we mated live warheads to our missiles. They were then directed at targets in Eastern Europe. Everything associated with the missiles, meaning their specifications and capabilities, was Top Secret at that time. I had a Secret Security Clearance, so I was authorized to work around the missiles, but could not know anything about them. I learned much later what they were capable of once the internet came about and the information about them had been de-classified. Previous to becoming a Pershing hot site, Kleingartach was used for Nike missiles.

The missile was 34.4 feet long, about 3.3 feet in diameter, and weighed 10,263 pounds. The warhead was 39 inches long and the missile was a solid propellant two-stage rocket. The missile's range was 460 miles, and it was considered intermediate field artillery. There were three levels of yield for the warheads meaning the level of destructive power, and they were 60 kilotons, 200 kilotons, and 400 kilotons. The type of warhead used was determined by the missile's target.

As an example, the two bombs dropped on Japan had yields of 13 kilotons (Hiroshima) and 21 kilotons (Nagasaki). Remember, we had 108 missiles in Germany. However, our military and political leaders never thought they would be used. They were referred to as Peacekeepers. The reason the warheads were so destructive (as I understand it) is because the guidance systems in the missiles were somewhat primitive. So, after a missile was launched it could drift off target one or more degrees. When traveling 460 miles that could be quite a distance off target. As such, the military decided the solution to the problem was to make the warheads more destructive.

The site was always occupied by a firing battery in the 3rd/84th with live warheads mated to the missiles. Within the 3rd/84th Field Artillery Battalion, there were six batteries –

Headquarters, Service, and four Firing Batteries: A, B, C, and D. Each firing battery would spend about 12 weeks there, then rotate out with another battery replacing it. Below is the technical explanation of the various stages of readiness of each battery and what the battalion required.

The schedule we kept meant we were located at Kleingartach once a year sometime around and during springtime. It also meant that during my tour we would relocate there three times.

M791 truck parked next to a Pershing 1a missile.

There were three phases to the Pershing System Cycle:

PERSHING SYSTEM CYCLE I

This cycle took place at Fort Redleg located near Heilbronn and was called the Maintenance Phase. The purpose of this phase was to service the Pershing system platform and equipment. This was also the period where leaves would be taken by crew members.

PERSHING SYSTEM CYCLE II

This cycle also took place at Fort Redleg and was called the Training Phase. During this period the crew was trained or if they were already familiar with the system – re-trained. They were instructed on how to use the system and how to work together. During this period, the battery was also providing general support, whether at Fort Redleg or during field maneuvers.

PERSHING SYSTEM CYCLE III

This cycle would include transferring the entire battery to Kleingartach CAS (Combat Alert Status) from Badnerhof and Fort Redleg. This would involve the current battery on status to begin dismantling missiles one at a time as the replacement battery brought their missiles online one at a time. The CAS period lasted for 12 weeks and the missiles were kept in firing position 24 hours a day.

As the warheads were mated to the missiles, each had to successfully complete a "Confidence Count" (which might take 3 – 4 hours) and then two "Quick Count" cycles (which would take 4 minutes). The Pershing's were then operationally ready and placed in standby mode. On the launch pads, tarps covered the missiles to protect them from the elements, and the guidance section was wrapped with a heated blanket to keep it at a warm stable temperature.

The PTS box (pictured above) was heated and air-conditioned to keep the computers at a warm stable temperature. The power station had a sliding door that closed off the exhaust port to protect it from the elements. The power plant was the same turbine engine that powered the UH1 Huey helicopter (1,100 hp Lycomb turbine engine).

Walter Gates, who provided all information regarding the missile cycles was a PTS Operator from Charlie Battery, 3rd Platoon, 3/84th FA Neckarsulm, from 1973-1974. He was also a B-Team member of the Warhead mating team. The Warhead mating team consisted of an A (an officer) and a B (an enlisted member).

His job duties in addition to running all the Counts included getting/entering the targeting data, testing the warhead electrical circuitry before mating to the missile (used a "magic box"), and mating the warhead to the missile (compressing the springs, plugging together the power/electrical cables between the guidance section and warhead, mounting the splice band, torquing the exploding bolts and connecting the electrical cables to the bolts releasing the locking pins on the compressed springs and snapping on the dust covers over the joints on the splice band).

The CAS site included an exclusion area and a controlled area. The exclusion area was surrounded by guard towers and a double fence topped with razor wire. Within the exclusion area was the following – the missiles set up on three separate firing pads with live warheads, warheads and ammunition bunkers, and a Battery Control Central (BCC) unit mounted on an M791 vehicle (similar to the M757 tractor). Shoot to kill was authorized within the exclusion area including any unauthorized attempt to gain access. The controlled area was surrounded by a single fence with a guarded gate. Within the controlled area were the dining facility, motor pool, missile maintenance, barracks, and administration offices. This complex was located about a half-mile from the exclusion area complex.

Each CAS firing pad was occupied by a firing platoon with their assigned missiles. Each missile was assigned a specific target. There were three CAS sites in Germany with six missiles each ready to fire on 18 different targets.

At night you could see where the exclusion site was relative to the controlled area because it was lit up like a prison. There were so many lights you could easily see the light above the treetops from this complex, which is where the motor pool lived (they were about a half-mile apart).

The exclusion area is where the missile crews lived. From what I understand, it was a very unpleasant experience for those guys. It was very hot in the summer, very cold in the winter, and it was rat-infested. In fact, it wasn't much more than a glorified garage. The guys that lived there (the firing platoons) were on call 24x7. Anytime the alarm sounded, it didn't matter what they were doing –sleeping, showering, eating, or just hanging out - they were required to run to their station and begin procedures for launching their missiles.

Lastly, there was a small Commo building a few hundred yards (right in the middle of farm fields) from the controlled area. This is where the communications platoon had their radar antenna inflated for use, which was to be in contact with Army Command. This area was also occupied 24 hours a day.

My first time in Kleingartach was the day after I arrived at Badnerhof Kaserne. Needless to say, as soon as I arrived with my buddy Henning, we found out we were leaving the next day and shouldn't bother to unpack. We were lost, confused, and clueless.

Devon in our living quarters in the Kleingartach admin building.

Holcum – wrecker driver in the Kleingartach motor pool bays.

THE GUARD SHACK AND MAJOR KELLEY

Shortly after arriving at the Admin Building (a secured complex) for the first time, I had to pull guard duty at the entrance. There was a fence around the perimeter and the only way in or out was through the gate and next to the gate was a guard shack where you'd sit until a vehicle approached the gate – either to enter or to leave. Then you'd open the gate to let the vehicle pass after verifying their identity if entering and that the driver had proper authorization to leave the post if exiting. From the very beginning of entering the military, you are taught to salute officers. Well, I was on my first round of guard duty and a jeep pulled up to enter the facility. I didn't notice that it had a plate on the front of the jeep indicating it was our Commanding Officer Major Kelley. I opened the gate and the jeep drove through about ten feet before stopping. The Major got out of the passenger side walked up to me, looked at my name tag on my shirt, and said, "Private Heyer – are you aware that you are supposed to salute an officer?" I said, "Yes sir!" He then saluted me. Remember, I'm supposed to salute him, not the other way around. He could have chewed me out, but he very kindly did not. However, he had made his point and I learned never to do that again.

The only time an officer salutes a subordinate (lower-ranking person) is if that subordinate has been awarded the Congressional Medal of Honor. This is the highest award anyone in the military can receive. In that case, even the highest-ranking general or admiral (Joint Chiefs of Staff included) is to salute that person – regardless of rank.

Back to the guard shack. There was a small hedgehog that lived in nearby bushes that would sneak up to the shack and eat any scraps of food it could find if your tray had been set on the ground outside of the shack especially at night.

The infamous guard shack at the entrance to the secured area (admin area) of Kleingartach.

KP (KITCHEN POLICE)

When I was new to the unit, I had to pull KP on at least one occasion – maybe two. This required getting up before everyone (around 0500 hours), reporting for duty, and working until about 2000 (twenty hundred) hours. The day consisted of running the dishwasher, washing pots and pans by hand, wiping down tables, and peeling potatoes. After each meal and everything had been cleaned you had about an hour to sit and chat with the cooks and other guys pulling KP until the next cycle started. It was exhausting.

MISSILE TRAILER ISSUES

There was a time when it became apparent to our command that the brakes on the missile trailers were locking up. Several mechanics went over to the missile site (exclusion area) to work on the trailers and we had to pass through two secured entrances with armed guards to gain access to the trailers.

Our job was to pull four huge tires/wheels from each of the nine trailers, inspect the brakes, and repair or replace them as necessary. Each of us took one trailer. What was rather intimidating was the fact that each missile was in its cradle with a live warhead mounted on it. Thankfully, the area with the tires (the back of the trailer) was located at the opposite end of the warhead.

The author standing in front of a P1a missile. I was working on the trailer and had to obtain authorization to take the photo because a live warhead was mated to the missile. I could take the pic from any angle as long as I did not include the right side of the warhead in the photo where stenciled on the warhead was its yield such as 60, 200, or 400 kilotons.

The entire warhead was surrounded by what looked like what only can be described as yellow crime scene tape. Located next to the missile was a small guard shack that was occupied by an infantryman with a loaded M16 whose job was to guard that warhead at all costs. If anyone unauthorized entered the taped off area, his orders were to protect the warhead up to and including the use of deadly force.

Infantryman guarding the warhead mated to the missile with Belt posing beside him. Notice the angle of the photograph shows the left side of the warhead, not the right. Also, the secured area around the warhead is identified by the tape.

VOLUNTEERING

Often there wasn't a lot for the motor pool staff to do when we were on status. That's what we called it when we lived at Kleingartach. I recall several times where I would offer to do various supply runs, driving back to Badnerhof to pick up parts or other needed items. I remember one time when Shorty and I offered to take the water truck – a 2 ½ ton truck with a couple of huge water tanks on the back – and fill them up at Badnerhof Kaserne which was our primary source of water. It was fun and would give us something to do rather than just sitting around in the motor pool office or the double bay area located next to the office.

Water truck (2 water pods strapped to the back of a 2 ½ ton truck) parked at Kleingartach in the motor pool lot. Notice the fire truck in the background. Our only vehicle that was not painted OD (olive drab) green.

HEAD INJURY

It was sometime in April of 1972 and it was a very windy day. At Kleingartach we had a building with the motor pool office and two bays attached to the office for working on trucks. Each bay had two heavy wooden doors that swung open to the outside. They were so tall that the latches at the top could only be reached with a six-foot-long heavy pole that had a loop on the far end for pushing up or pulling down the latch at the top. We always left the pole hanging on one of the latches.

One day we held the doors open to one bay so a truck could back out. I was holding one of the doors (the one with the pole on it) and someone else was holding the other. The wind was so strong that it pulled the door out of my hands and slammed it against the outside wall. In doing so, the pole flew off the hook and the blunt end of it hit me in the head, almost knocking me out. I had a cut on my head that was bleeding profusely, and I looked like I had just been in battle. I was so confused and dazed by the impact of the rod, I wandered into the office and began looking for something though to this day I do not know what I was looking for.

I needed medical treatment so Peewee escorted me to the medic's office where ultimately, I needed three stitches in my head. I had terrible headaches for several days but I'm lucky the pole didn't penetrate my skull. To this day, I can find the spot on my head where it hit me.

WILLIAMS AND OMELETS

At Kleingartach the menu of the day was posted on Sundays and one of the breakfast options was always an omelet made to order. Williams was the cook and when Hester asked for an omelet, Williams would reply, "what is your order?" Again, Hester asked for an omelet and Williams again asked, "what is your order?" Hester then proceeded to tell Williams that a made to order omelet was an option on the menu posted at the entrance to the mess hall. Williams replied that he didn't have enough staff to do that. So, on Sunday mornings Hester started getting up early, going downstairs to the mess hall, and would help in the kitchen by cutting up various vegetables and meats that could be used in an omelet. It was nice of him to do that. I do recall having an omelet and they were very good.

L to R: McKendree, Williams, and Findley.

BATTALION COMMANDER'S HELICOPTER

The way our Battalion Commander (located at Neckarsulm, Germany) visited Kleingartach was via his Bell UH-1 Huey helicopter. Whenever he visited, his pilots had nothing to do, so they were authorized to take us for rides if anyone was interested. Hester and I decided to take a ride and it was pretty wild. The pilots would take you up about 500 feet and fly around the area, performing awesome flight maneuvers. The craziest part was that we would sit on the side of the chopper (in seats with a seat belt on), however, the pilots left the doors open so we could hang outside the chopper to take pictures. I don't think I would do something like that today because I would be too scared (or smart).

Battalion Commander's Bell UH-1 Huey parked outside the Admin Bldg site at Kleingartach.

Huey Specs (UH-1D):

Crew: 1–4
Length: 57 feet, 1 in (17.40 m) with rotors

Width:	8 feet, 7 in (2.62 m) (fuselage)
Height:	14 feet, 5 in (4.39 m)
Empty weight:	5,215 pounds (2,365 kg)
Gross weight:	9,040 pounds (4,100 kg)
Capacity:	3,880 pounds (1,760 kg) including 14 troops, or 6 stretchers, or equivalent cargo

The author sitting in our battalion commander's helicopter getting ready for a ride.

HARRISON'S CAR

Another guy in the motor pool, Harrison, had a father who was an officer somewhere in Europe. Harrison was married and lived off post, so he had a car – a nice Volkswagen station wagon. Somehow Harrison got into an accident, but we were never really clear on what happened. Connors (our tow truck driver) went and retrieved the car with Harrison.

Connors retrieving Harrison's damaged car with the motor pool's 5-ton wrecker.

For some reason, Harrison did not want his dad to know what had happened to the car. At least that's what he told us. So, rather than having the car repaired, he asked us to cut up the car and throw it away. Seriously! We all took turns using the motor pool's blow torch, cut it up, and tossed the pieces in the dumpster. We all shook our heads over that one and never did understand why.

Not only did I learn how to use a cutting torch in the Army, but I also learned how to weld. I wasn't the best, but I could get by. Because welding rods were so difficult to come by, we used coat hangers instead. They seemed to work fine, and the welds always held.

Harrison's car in the process of being cut up with a blow torch.

FATAL AUTO ACCIDENT

One of the saddest drinking incidents was a fatal accident with two guys in A Battery. It was a weekend at Kleingartach in May of 1972 and there had been drinking in the NCO club, where we played cards (hearts and spades), foosball, and watched movies. Well, two guys decided they wanted to go to a nearby town for more drinking at a German Gasthaus. The driver, Spec 5 Crown, had just re-enlisted and bought a brand new 1972 Gran Torino with a portion ($3,200) of the $5,000 he had received as a re-enlistment bonus.

The passenger was a guy by the name of Griffon and a good friend of mine, and he had just married his sweetheart in the states the Christmas before. They asked if others wanted to go – including me – but we all turned them down. Unfortunately, no one stopped them. They left with another car (a Mach 1 Mustang) that was owned by the supply sergeant. They were traveling at a very high rate of speed on backcountry roads, racing with the Mustang, which followed behind the Gran Torino, and hit the side of a stone building. I'm sure the guys in the Mustang were incredibly traumatized when they drove up on the accident. Neither Crown nor Griffon was wearing a seatbelt. My buddy Griffon was killed instantly (it's my understanding that he ended up under the dashboard on the driver's side under Crown's legs) and Crown survived long enough to be transported to the hospital where Top McCarthy visited him, but he later died of his injuries.

I was deeply troubled by this incident. The flag at Kleingartach was flown at half-staff for several days because of their deaths. The totaled car was on display at the entrance to battalion headquarters at Neckasrulm Kaserne for several weeks. I eventually obtained donations from anyone who wanted to give and sent flowers to both families in the U.S. I have several photos in my albums of the car. Very tragic.

Sp 5 Crown's 1972 Gran Torino. Griffon was a passenger in this car.

Griffon – One of our cooks and a good friend of mine.

Flag at Kleingartach in front of Admin building at half-staff because of the deaths of Griffon and Crown.

F4 PHANTOM JETS

The Air Force used the Admin Area (secured area) for practicing strafing runs. At the time, the F4 Phantom was probably the Air Force's most amazing fighter jet. I'm proud to say it was manufactured in St. Louis by McDonnell-Douglas. The pilots loved to fly over us at what seemed like full throttle just above the treetops. Literally, they would almost blow out our eardrums they were so loud, but it was awesome to see and to hear. The F4 specs are listed below (including a photo).

F4 Phantom Jet Specs:
Length: 58.3 feet
Height: 16.6 feet
Wingspan: 38.5 feet
Weight: 55,597 pounds (25,200kg)
Max takeoff weight: 60,000 pounds (27,000kg)
Max speed: 1,485mph (2,309kmph)
Range: 1,750 miles (2,816km)

A SUNDAY WALK IN THE FOREST

One Sunday during my first 12-week visit to Kleingartach, several of us decided to walk to a nearby town. It was probably located a couple of miles away and we took a short cut through a beautiful forest. Once we got to the clearing, you could see a castle located on a hill overlooking the town. Someone in the group figured (or somehow knew) it was from the 11th century. I don't know what we were thinking, but we thought we had the right to walk right up to the castle and past it as we worked our way into town. It was obvious someone lived there, because there was a car parked right in front of the entrance. We were trespassing by walking on their property, but we didn't seem to give it a second thought.

CHAPTER EIGHT
NECKARSULM KASERNE, NECKARSULM, GERMANY

Neckarsulm, a smaller neighboring town of Heilbronn, was where our battalion headquarters (3rd/84th) was located. You could drive from one Kaserne to the other in about 15-20 minutes. I have a few memories of this Kaserne, but not as many as Badnerhof. The car Griffon was killed in was placed at the entrance to Neckarsulm Kaserne for everyone to see and was kept there for several weeks. It was very sobering to have it there on display.

AMMO DUMP AND GUARD DUTY

During Thanksgiving 1971 I had to pull 24-hour guard duty at the ammo dump located adjacent to Neckarsulm Barracks, where munitions including the nuclear warheads were stored when not mated to the missiles. I was already homesick, so this just seemed to add to that feeling. The complex was secured with fencing and razor wire at the top and there were four guard towers – one located at each corner of the complex. The rotation consisted of two hours of guard duty and four hours off.

Obviously, it was quite cold in late November and the towers at that time were in terrible shape.

They were made of plywood that required you to climb a ladder and enter the tower through the floor of the shack. Where Plexiglas should have been, there was nothing and they were not heated. The only nice part of the experience was that we were transported to Neckarsulm Barracks in the evening so we could enjoy a Thanksgiving dinner.

Later, I would have guard duty one more time there before being promoted to a sergeant, whereby you no longer pulled guard duty or KP. The second time on guard duty was much better. The old towers had been replaced with new steel towers that were properly enclosed, heated and you entered by climbing a stairway and entering the tower from the side through a door. However, it still was not fun – two hours on and four hours off for 24 long hours of guard duty.

GUN INCIDENT

My buddy, Babich, who was our mail clerk, was picking up A Battery's mail at battalion headquarters and somehow got into a heated discussion with several soldiers who were sitting on the steps leading into the building. One soldier was carrying an unauthorized handgun (a starter gun that shot caps or blanks) and pulled it on Babich. He fired it at his arm and the pistol was close enough to his arm that the black powder burned through his fatigue shirt and burned his skin. He was advised by the assailants not to say anything, but he did anyway, mostly because he needed medical treatment and because he was very angry. The result was the guy who fired the pistol was demoted to private and given a monetary fine. Based on the punishment, I would assume he was given an Article 15 for assault.

OUT OF UNIFORM

One day while we were at Kleingartach I volunteered to run to battalion headquarters for Top McCarthy. That morning I put on a civilian shirt under my fatigues (olive drab working clothes). You could barely see the shirt under my uniform, but it was noticeable if you were paying attention. I was walking along the sidewalk at Battalion Headquarters and passed an officer (I knew the importance of saluting by this time) and the officer noticed my civilian shirt peeking out from under my uniform. Needless to say, he let me have it with both barrels. I was an NCO (a sergeant!) and I was out of uniform. I believe he threatened to put me on report. Thank God he didn't, and I never did that again. To this day, I don't know why Top McCarthy didn't say something to me about it (I wish he had), however, at the end of the day it was my responsibility to be in uniform and I was not.

MOVING TO NECKARSULM

In the spring of 1973, the decision was made to rehab A Battery's building at Badnerhof. As a result, we all had to relocate to Neckarsulm and were spread out among several buildings. The motor pool was located on the 4th floor of one of the barracks, and since Shorty and I were sergeants, we had our own room. The rest of the guys lived in a huge bay area located next to our room.

A FIRE IN THE BARRACKS

Because I was rotating out of the Army in a few months, I bought some civilian clothes and stored them in my wall locker along with my military uniforms and personal effects, including my high school jacket from Vianney. Sometime early on a new mechanic joined the motor pool. He was different and a little strange. Little did we know how different. For whatever reason, he did not like Shorty or me.

One day while we were out (probably at work), he lit matches and dropped them through the top slats of our wall lockers, setting both on fire. Subsequently, the building began to fill with smoke. Babich was the first to notice the fire and ran to our Battery officers to inform them he needed a gas mask because the smoke was so thick – they also called the fire department. He got a gas mask from the armory and used it and a nearby extinguisher to have the fire mostly extinguished by the time the fire department arrived.

The fires were extinguished before they did too much damage, but the contents of both lockers were destroyed – either by the fire or the water used to extinguish it. I don't know what happened to the guy, but he was transferred somewhere immediately – maybe a psych ward. We lost all of our clothes and everything else in our lockers and had to get everything reissued to us. We also were given some money to replace the non-military clothes we had lost, but both of us were angry. The only thing I salvaged from the contents was a "70" patch on my high school jacket – the year I graduated.

THE HESTERS LIVING ON THE ECONOMY

When we moved to Neckarsulm, I had all my stereo equipment and albums to contend with. Since my tour would not end for another five or six months, I couldn't ship them home for free yet. So, I stored them at Hester's house. Linda didn't have a television and loved having the music, plus I had a place to store them until I finished my tour.

COMMISSARY

During the last few months that Shorty and I were in Germany, we could no longer stomach the food at the mess hall. It's not that it was bad, we just couldn't eat the same food over and over and over again. The breakfast was fine. It was lunch and dinner that was the issue. We started eating at the Commissary lunch area for those two meals and pretty much did so for our remaining time.

MANEUVERS

In September, A Battery was scheduled to go to Graefenfoehr for training for about three weeks. Because I was rotating out the next month and would be ending my tour of duty, I didn't have to go. When all the vehicles lined up for the 14-hour convoy drive in the quadrangle between all of the buildings, I stood outside and watched them prepare to leave. It was the weirdest feeling I'd had since joining the Army. The unit I was part of for more than 2-½ years was leaving without me and so it was the first time I no longer felt like I was part of the unit. I was happy that I was going home soon but very sad that I felt the way I did.

CHAPTER NINE
WHARTON BARRACKS, HEILBRONN

The other military post in Heilbronn was Wharton Barracks. This facility was larger than Badnerhof and not only included medical buildings, finance offices, and other administration offices, it included military housing for Officers and NCO's that were career soldiers located next to it. This is where I had to go if I had a doctor or dentist appointment. In fact, this is where I went to have bridgework done on my mouth.

I had two dental problems as a kid. One involved a chipped front tooth while shooting bb guns with a neighborhood friend. We were shooting at each other and as I cocked the gun to fire it, it slipped from my hand and popped me in the mouth. I really got in trouble with my mom for that one. The second was that I was born with a permanent tooth that wouldn't come in. Eventually, it had to be pulled and I had a fake tooth instead. I was always breaking the fake tooth, so while I was in the Army, I thought I would have the necessary dental work performed to have a bridge installed.

What I didn't realize was that the dentist performing the procedure was learning his trade and I was one of his guinea pigs. For about eighteen months he worked on my mouth from time to time – grinding down teeth and having me wear temporary crowns. He never used enough medicine to deaden the nerves, so it always hurt to the point of tears running down my cheeks as he would grind away.

As I neared the end of my tour, I was at an appointment and informed him that I would be getting out in a couple of months and he replied that he didn't think he could complete the work before then. I was so lucky because right after he made that statement his boss (a colonel) was touring the facility and asked what I was having done. I took that opportunity to explain the conversation the dentist and I had just had. The colonel quickly informed the dentist (basically ordering him) that he would finish the work on my teeth before I rotated back to the states. When I finally left Germany, I had a new permanent bridge, however, he still hadn't permanently glued it in place, so I had to have that done after I got out.

CHAPTER TEN
REDLEG, CAS/ TRAINING SITE OUTSIDE OF HEILBRONN

This was a training site located about 15 minutes from Badnerhof Kaserne. The firing platoons go through three stages of readiness with the missiles and stages one and two were performed at Redleg, and stage three was at the CAS site location in Kleingartach.

M757 Tractor pulling an EL (Erector Launcher) trailer with Pershing Missile at Redleg. The warhead could be stored in a separate container adjacent to the missile.

PICNIC

The first summer I was in Heilbronn, there was a BBQ held at Redleg which included booths, food, and various rides. My Commanding Officer, Major Kelley, was in a dunking booth and I managed to hit the paddle with a ball causing him to fall into the water. I was the first (and I believe the only) one that sent him into the water. We both laughed about it and as a result, I bought him a beer. There were very few women at the picnic, which was odd, but it was likely only the wives of those who were married and living in Heilbronn were in attendance.

MANEUVERS

I recall one summer we were on maneuvers and used the Redleg site. During maneuvers, the firing batteries ran simulated countdowns to launch the missiles and they would do this over and over again. We spent the night there and slept out under the stars. What was interesting about this outing was that Redleg was also an airfield for helicopters. As such, while we were sleeping, I recall helicopters flying in and out several times throughout the night. And obviously, they were very loud. It sounded as though they were just above the trees flying right over us. As a result, we didn't get much sleep for the two nights we were there.

SHORTY AND THE GLOW PLUG

Anytime A Battery was working at Redleg it was in preparation for a move to Kleingartach. It was winter and we had just made the move, however, we had a broken down M757 tractor that had been left behind. Shorty and I took the motor pool's wrecker to either get the tractor started or tow it to Kleingartach. Unlike gasoline-powered engines, diesel engines do not have spark plugs that ignite the fuel. Instead, the compression in a diesel engine's cylinders is so high that the compression itself causes the fuel/air mixture to ignite.

One downfall to this is that diesel engines require assistance when starting them in cold weather which is accomplished by warming the fuel before it enters the combustion chamber. This happens with a glow plug, which is screwed into the intake manifold. The fuel is heated when you push a button on the dashboard causing the plug to glow inside the manifold. The first thing we did was to check the tractor's plug to make sure it worked properly with Shorty in the driver's seat and me in the passenger seat and the huge six-cylinder engine located in the compartment between us in the cab.

Shorty unscrewed the spark plug from the manifold and left it attached to the plug wire. He held it in his right hand while he pressed the ignitor switch button on the dashboard with his left. Guess what? The plug worked! However, the electricity (24 volts) burned his right hand. It was hilarious. The funniest part was that once was not enough. He pressed it again! We both couldn't stop laughing. To this day, I laugh when I think about it. I believe we ended up towing the M757 to Kleingartach because we couldn't get it started.

In the Army, when jump-starting one vehicle using another a freedom cable is used (this is a term used by the military). They are much more convenient than typical jumper cables because you don't attach them directly to the batteries. Rather, the cable (male end) is plugged into a receptacle (female end) mounted on the exterior of each vehicle, thus there is no need to access the batteries directly, which can be located in difficult to reach areas.

CHAPTER ELEVEN
GRAFENWOEHR (GRAF) TRAINING SITE

During WWII, this site was used by Hitler's deadly, fanatical SS troops for training purposes. After the war, the U.S. Army used it for training purposes as well. In March of 1972, A Battery (all 86 vehicles) traveled in a 14-hour convoy to Graf (a slang term we used for the site). It was a huge complex located near the Czechoslovakian border on the far east side of West Germany.

Our convoy en route to Graf stopped along the Autobahn.

We left Redleg before light. I was in the tool truck with Krakowski and we took turns driving and riding shotgun. We rode together for several hours though at some point (I don't know why) I ended up riding in the back of Lt. White's jeep. I also recall that whoever was driving the jeep eventually got lost and we thought we might end up at the Czech border. Eventually, we were able to get back on course and found the complex.

It was so large that artillery guns and tanks could fire their weapons to practice shooting at targets. During our three weeks there, it seemed like there was always a war going on. The sound of artillery fire was constant and went on day and night, rain or shine. The reason we went there for training purposes was that our commanders wanted to prove that Pershing could function in any kind of weather and be successful in performing its mission even under the most adverse conditions. It was freezing the entire time and the wind seemed to be always blowing. The area was open with no vegetation where the vehicles were parked so the wind just went right through you. It was the rifle ranges during basic training all over again.

We lived in long, narrow concrete barracks with a potbelly stove in the middle for heat. We slept on bunks, but in our sleeping bags – and often in our clothes. During the day, we were out in the field trying to keep the trucks running. I recall these massive tanks passing us on the roads – M-60 Patton tanks – and there was no room for both of us on the road, so one or the other had to move to the side – generally, it was the tanks. They were something to see and hear. Below are a photo and the specifications of the M-60 Patton tank.

M-60 Patton Tank Specs:
Weight:	60 tons
Length:	32 feet, 4 inches
Width:	13 feet, 6 inches
Height:	12 feet, 6 inches
Ground clearance:	18 inches
Track width:	28 inches
Forward speed:	30 mph
Reverse speed:	10 mph
Vertical obstacle climb:	49 inches
Maximum width ditch:	108 inches
Fording depth:	48 inches
Guns:	
Main:	105mm/ 51cal M68 rifled gun (63 rounds)
Coaxial:	M240 – 7.62mm (5,950 rounds)
Commander:	M85 - .50cal antiaircraft gun (900 rounds)

L to R: Krakowski, Belt, and Summers hanging out in our barracks. We are bundled up indoors because it was so cold.

I was still assigned to the Commo platoon but was allowed to spend almost all of my time with the motor pool guys including where I slept, which was much appreciated.

One of the few other details I recall from Graf was the shower, toilet, and shaving facilities were the same as what I experienced at Ft. Leonard Wood living in the old WWII barracks. Just as before it was a little embarrassing to have such a lack of privacy when using the toilet.

SOUVENIERS

We all left Graf with souvenirs. Some guys bought lighters and had them engraved. I had been given a lighter when I entered the Army from some close friends, and they had "Shorttimer Oct' 1973" engraved on one side and "Michael Heyer" engraved on the other. I had "FTA" engraved on one side and "Graf" engraved on the other. I still have this lighter today.

Another popular souvenir was 155mm spent shells. They were huge. I believe they were about 2-½' long and about 6" in diameter. Many of us brought one back with us thinking we could ship them home. After returning to Badnerhof we quickly learned that even though they were spent shells, they were in fact munitions, and thus were not eligible to be shipped back to the states.

Photo of the author holding a 155mm shell casing.

CHAPTER TWELVE
VEHICLE TRIPS AND MISHAPS

Throughout my time in Germany, several vehicle mishaps happened. There are also pleasant and amusing memories that I can relate to vehicles. The ones mentioned here didn't fit anywhere else.

Shorty driving motor pool wrecker pulling a broken-down deuce and half at Redleg. Note: he was pulling a wheelie. The stencil - 7A3F84 on the right side of the bumper indicates 7 Army, 3rd Battalion 84th Field Artillery. On the left side of the bumper, A33 indicates A Battery truck number 33.

HOOD MISHAP

Another time Hester and I were running an errand and we had the motor pool's 5/4-ton truck A61. I was driving and Hester was in the passenger seat as we drove down a long straight country road that ran between the town of Kleingartach and Heilbronn. The speed limit was about 45 mph (roughly 72 KPH). The way this vehicle's hood is secured is two spring-loaded latches (one on each side).

What we didn't know is that someone had undone the latches and not put them back. As I got up to speed the wind caught under the hood and raised it, blocking our view through the windshield. The road was busy and there was a fair amount of traffic moving in both directions. Fortunately, we both thought very fast and stuck our heads out of the truck (thank God the windows were down). I also took my foot off the gas and began braking until we slowed down enough to pull off onto the shoulder where we properly re-attached the latches. Needless to say, that incident scared the hell out of us and we never figured out who the numbskull was that left the latches unsecured.

BABICH'S ACCIDENT

I went home on leave in May of 1972. While I was home, Babich and another guy were in a serious truck accident. Ironically, it was only one week after Babich arrived in the unit. They were making a run between Badnerhof and Redleg. They were traveling in a 5/4-ton truck and were catapulted off the road, careening across oncoming traffic before finally slamming into a tree. Fortunately, they did not hit anyone head-on. However, the driver's pelvis was fractured, and he had other broken bones, but I do not recall what they were. I heard that because of his pelvic fracture, he had to learn to walk again. I never saw him again.

Babich was riding in the passenger seat and his left forearm was shattered. In the end, he needed to have metal plates put in his arm. I believe they are still there to this day. His arm was shattered because the two batteries in this vehicle are in a huge square box located between the driver's and passenger's seat and his arm hit that metal box. And don't forget that military vehicles did not have seat belts at that time.

The cause of the accident was later determined to be a propeller shaft (drive shaft) that ran from the front differential axle (PTO or power takeoff) to a winch located on the front of the truck. The connection with the bearings was broken (u joint) and rather than remove the shaft (which would have been the proper thing to do) some idiot tied it up with wire. Eventually, the wire wore away from the spinning shaft. When it did it dropped down with the broken end hitting the ground and launching the vehicle into the air. This accident should not have happened at all. There was an investigation trying to determine who performed such a thoughtless act. However, it could never be determined as to who did it so, the matter was dropped.

The 5/4-ton truck in which Babich was riding.

CROSSING THE HIGHWAY

I recall one incident with our motor pool five-ton wrecker. Hill was out on a very late-night run that involved picking up a broken-down deuce and a half. The trip included driving on the Autobahn (where the idea for the U.S. highway system was born during WWII) and as he was driving back, the towing bar broke. The towing bar could be used instead of the cable and hook arrangement to tow a vehicle. In fact, you should use the towing bar whether or not you are using the cable and hook. When the towing bar broke it resulted in the towed vehicle separating from the tow truck. It crossed the median, then the oncoming traffic lanes until it finally wound up off the road on the other side of the highway. Thank God it was late at night otherwise the truck might have hit oncoming vehicles, which almost surely would have resulted in fatalities.

HEILBRONN'S NARROW BACK STREETS

I remember driving on the back streets of Heilbronn on many occasions. Since German towns are much older than in the U.S. and their vehicles are generally much smaller than American vehicles, the roads were naturally much narrower than streets in the U.S.

There was one specific occasion where I was driving an M757 tractor deadhead (absent a trailer). I was tooling along and for whatever reason had to go down a narrow street. I was moving along about 20 mph but felt like I was flying down the road, because there was such little clearance on either side of the road and because cars were parked on both sides of the road. I probably should have slowed down, but I just wasn't thinking very responsibly.

CONNORS AND A STOP SIGN (HALT)

Connors was driving and Hester was riding in the motor pool's five-ton wrecker while they were pulling another broken down wrecker. The plan was to return to Kleingartach after picking up the wrecker and they were going the back way which required a very tight turn at some point during the return trip.

It just so happened that a 10-year-old German boy happened to be around that turn and was waving at vehicles as they passed by. Connors was trying to navigate the tight turn, which included avoiding a stop sign, and on his first try was unable to make it. He backed up to widen the turn and that didn't work either. After several tries, he became frustrated and just drove on. In doing so, the rear wheels of the towed wrecker ran over the stop sign flattening it on the ground.

The little boy must have witnessed the event and went home to tell his parents because when Connors and Hester arrived at Kleingartach's secured area the Polizzi (police) were already there and waiting. The accident cost several hundred marks in damages, however, rather than replace the sign, the Germans brought their street crew who heated the base of the signpost where it was bent with a blow torch and then raised it and straightened it. Naturally, it didn't take several hundred dollars to repair the sign.

2-½ TON TRUCK WITH REAR AXLE KNOCKED OUT OF ALIGNMENT

Someone (I don't recall who) had driven a deuce and a half and somehow hit a very tough obstruction. In doing so, they knocked the forward rear axle out of alignment (there was no other damage to the vehicle). In other words that axle and the four tires on it were not perpendicular to the truck frame. We never did hear what the driver hit, but it must have been something permanent. I had never seen an axle out of alignment in that way before and never saw one again.

ROLLING TRUCK AND A GERMAN SHED

Shortly, after I had arrived at A Battery and had returned from my first trip to Kleingartach, there was an incident on the motor pool lot. One of our deuce and a half trucks was parked on the edge of the lot with its back end facing the perimeter fence. Just outside of the fence was the backyard of a German civilian with a shed at the end of his lot. Somehow after the driver had parked the truck, he had not properly parked it in gear and used chock blocks under the rear wheels. As a result, the truck rolled off the lot, down the slight incline through the perimeter fence running into and destroying the German's tool shed.

A German neighbor's backyard tool shed was damaged when a 2-½ ton truck rolled off the motor pool lot and down the hill.

ROAD TRIP TO RAMSTEIN

On another occasion, I rode with Peewee to take two mechanics rotating back to the states to Ramstein Air Base outside Frankfurt. Before being assigned to A Battery, they were both stationed in Vietnam and were in the 101st Airborne. Peewee had a late model Mercury with a high-performance 351 cubic inch engine which he obtained from a totaled car (it had been rear-ended) at Wharton Barracks.

On our return trip, Peewee decided to see what his new engine could do, and he had it up to 145 mph on the Autobahn.

We were tooling along just fine until a car pulled out into the left lane to pass another car. We almost went into the guard rail on the left side of the lane and I was so scared that I lost my breath. I don't recall if there were seat belts in the car but if there were, we weren't wearing them. He slowed down to about 90 after that.

BREAKDOWN ON THE AUTOBAHN

I recall a trip not long after I had arrived in Heilbronn where Donnelson was driving our 5/4-ton truck. I believe we had been to the can yard to obtain some part for a broken down A Battery vehicle. If my recollection is accurate, we had a cooling system issue such as a blown radiator hose, bad water pump, or radiator leak.

Because there were no cell phones, our only option was to walk to the nearest gas station or stop at a house along the autobahn. Donnelson was a really nice guy but was a bit shy and very introverted and did not want to try either one of those options. And I didn't feel like I could argue because I was new. He thought we should just stay in the truck and eventually someone would come to find us. The one downside was that it was fall and it got pretty cool after the sun went down.

Donnelson was correct though. Eventually, at about 0100 hours our wrecker passed us, pulled off the autobahn, and backed up to hook us up to the truck. It was Peewee coming to our rescue. We later found out that after we didn't return when they had expected us, they figured something was wrong and retraced the route we would have taken.

A NEW WRECKER

I recall at one point we received a new 5-ton wrecker. It was a Dodge vehicle and had a Cummins diesel engine, which has a distinct sound as if the lifters are about to rattle apart inside the engine (or they are not getting enough lubricant). It was a beautiful vehicle.

OUR VW BUG

In preparation for our trip to Le Mans in June of 1973, Babich, Shorty, and I purchased a VW bug from someone rotating back to the states. It needed a little work but was in relatively good shape. The plan was to use the car for our trip, then give it to Hester and his new bride as a wedding gift. Hester had gone back to the states (Dublin, GA) to marry Linda (whom he is still married to) and bring her back to Germany. They planned to live on the economy in a small neighboring town and would need transportation, so it worked out perfectly for all of us.

THE GENERATOR INCIDENT

Probably the funniest vehicle story I have involves Hester and the can yard (which I believe was located in Kaiserslautern). Whenever you made a trip to the can yard, you had to have an officer sign off not only on taking a military vehicle off post (this was needed anytime you did that), but also to have requisitions signed by your motor officer authorizing you to obtain specific parts at the can yard.

Hester and I didn't want to bother with the hassle of that part of the process, so we just drove there intending to enter the enclosed yard during the lunch hour when no one was around. We would then take whatever we needed, and no one would be the wiser. We didn't think we were stealing because we were taking from another Army unit to help our Army unit. We arrived at the can yard when we intended and began our search. The primary reason for our trip was to find a generator for a deuce and a half.

Well there wasn't a deuce and a half in the can yard, however, some deuce and a half driver had parked his perfectly operational truck right outside the can yard and he had more than likely gone to lunch. Hester and I looked at each other and discussed how quickly we thought we could remove a generator. Three bolts held it in place – two underneath mounted to the engine block and one on top attaching it to an adjustable arm so you could control the tension on the belt that turned the pulley on the generator. Plus, a cable attached to it that connects to the batteries.

Ultimately, it required someone underneath in the wheel well and someone on top of the fender working under the hood. We decided we could have that generator off that truck in less than five minutes and be on our way. So, Hester climbed up on the hood and I worked my way into the wheel well. We removed that generator in record time, then jumped into our truck and took off. At the time, we were both sergeants and would have been busted had we been caught. I felt sorry for the driver and can't imagine what went through his mind when he returned to his truck with the hood up and his generator missing. What we did was a bit crazy!

TRANSPORTED BY A CHINOOK

Earlier in this memoir, I talked about having to re-qualify with our M16 each year and how we would fly in two CH47 Chinook helicopters to get to the training site. Chinook helicopters are an amazing workhorse for the Army as they can transport troops (up to 44 soldiers and crew) or vehicles, and riding in them is an awesome experience.

They have two large rotors (three blades each) that raise them off the ground and two turbine engines that propel them forward. You enter from the rear and when they're flying the tailgate can either be up or down so you can see out. You are seated on both sides from front to back, but while flying, you can't carry on a conversation – even with the person sitting next to you, because they are incredibly loud. I want to say that we went to the ranges sometime in early August of 1971.

TRAGIC LOSS

About two weeks after we used those two choppers, one of them crashed and everyone on board was killed – about 37 guys – soldiers and crew who were from a Pershing Unit located in Neu Ulm. The date was August 18, 1971. It was extremely sad as these were guys just like me and my buddies. Many years later, an unconfirmed report indicated that a faulty rotor blade was removed and turned into the supply system. The rotor blade then reportedly was incorrectly re-entered into the supply system as serviceable, returned, and installed back on the aircraft.

In other words, this accident was due to human error. Then during flight, the rear rotor blade broke free and struck the helicopter causing structural failure. The CH47 broke into two parts and crashed in a hayfield near Pegnitz, West Germany with the complete loss of life including four members of the flight crew. I believe there is a plaque at the site of the crash honoring all who lost their lives.

A CH47 Chinook Helicopter in flight.

CH47 Chinook Helicopter specs:
Rotor Diameter: 60 feet
Height: 18 feet, 7.8 inches
Fuselage Width: 12 feet, 5 inches
Fuel Capacity: 1,034 gallons
Maximum Speed: 189mph

Mechanics in A Battery didn't wear our dog tags when on duty. That is because when we worked on vehicles (primarily leaning over a running engine) there was a risk that our tags could fall out of our shirt at the neckline and get caught in a fan blade or belt. However, after this accident, there was a directive from the brigade command that dog tags were to be worn at all times. We figured that directive came down because there must have been soldiers on that helicopter that were not wearing their dog tags.

CHAPTER THIRTEEN
HEILBRONN, GERMANY – THE TOWN

On weekends, we were free to go into town provided we didn't have any kind of duty to perform. For the guys who lived off post because they were married, it was called living on the economy. Anyway, we could walk to town or take the bus, since most of the time we were there, no one owned a car. I loved going into town. The Germans were friendly, and it was nice to be off a military post for a short time.

OKTOBERFEST

One of our favorite times was during Oktoberfest which was located in town near the train station. Huge beer garden tents were set up and there were also arcade booths, food booths, and carnival rides to enjoy. It was a lot of fun mingling with the Germans and there were lots of pretty girls to see. I never drank more than a liter of beer at a time, except the one time I mentioned earlier about then getting on the Western Roundup ride.

THE WESTERN STORE

The Western store was geared toward American clothes such as jeans, shirts, jackets, and shoes – especially boots and other western-style accessories – belts, belt buckles, etc. It was located behind Wharton Barracks on the edge of town and was fun to visit. You felt like you were in an American store even though it was owned and run by Germans.

ROCK CONCERTS IN THE PARK

Badnerhof Kaserne was located just up the hill from Heilbronn's Park which was a nice park and probably about as big as Kirkwood Park. There were often rock concerts performed in the park and we would go listen to the various groups that would perform American rock music. The park would be crowded with many young Germans and American Soldiers. What I was not used to was the liberal nature of the young ladies. In the men's restroom, there was a wall that ran along one entire side opposite the stalls where you would relieve yourself. Well while I was standing there, ladies would invariably come in to use the stalls and not think anything of it.

During my tour, I did attend one rock concert with a few other guys in Mannheim. We went to see Three Dog Night. Their warmup band was Bertha whose lead singer was a rather large lady, and they were very good. It was so much fun seeing

Three Dog Night. I had seen them one other time in St. Louis in 1968. At that time, they were the warmup band for Steppenwolf.

Music festival at Heilbronn's park.

VOLKSMARCHES

The Germans have a very nice custom of taking walks through forests that are located just outside of town. They had long, wide paths that wound through beautiful forests that looked as though they were out of a fairytale. The walks were generally 3K or 5K in length and after you completed the walk, you would receive a medal for your accomplishment. I collected several while I was there.

THE WORLD'S OLDEST PROFESSION

Prostitution was legal in Germany. When I first got there the prostitutes would stand on a street in front of a huge electronics company – AEG Telefunken. The street was referred to as Telefunken Strasse. We went there once or twice out of curiosity, but that was all. Later a house was opened within the downtown area. When we heard of it, we thought we should at least go see what it looked like. Again, I was not going there as a customer, but rather out of curiosity.

I was not interested in having sex with a stranger. I was saving myself for that special person someday. However, just to be safe, I did not bring any money with me. It was a pretty amazing experience to just walk through it. There were several floors, and you could just walk on through going up and down the stairs. On each floor, there were several bedrooms with beautiful, scantily clad young ladies sitting outside the rooms and many holding little dogs for companions in their lap. There were also several bouncers walking throughout with German Shepherds on leashes to prevent any trouble. I only walked through one time, but it was an experience I never forgot.

There was a house in Stuttgart as well called House of 3 Colors. We heard that if you were taking a cab there that all you had to do was to tell the driver the address (which was 221) and they knew where to take you.

WORKING AT THE LOCAL VW DEALER

The summer before I finished my tour the Army established a new program that allowed those of us who had done well to work in a civilian job that we thought would be similar to what we would do after we got out. Shorty and I were the first to participate from A Battery and we both got jobs as mechanics with the local VW dealer for 60 days. In the beginning, we were each assigned to a mechanic and my guy's name was Mr. Pater. The German greeting that folks sometimes give in the morning is guten Morgen meaning Good Morning! The shortened version is to just say, Morgen! One of my fond memories, though there are many, is that morning greeting. It felt very welcoming. Shorty's assigned mechanic (I don't recall his name) had a 914 Porsche and used to let Shorty drive it. In fact, we visited the guy in his apartment because he and Shorty had become such good friends.

Most of the mechanics were older and didn't trust us because they knew nothing about us. In time, they began to trust us and allowed us to do more hands-on repairs. One of the limitations was that they did not speak English and we spoke very little German, but we managed to get by. The younger workers were excited to try out their English on us as they had been learning it in school as their second language. Of course, they wanted to try out all the cuss words they had learned as well.

Another interesting aspect of working there was that workers could drink beer during lunch and would buy it out of old coin-operated coke machines. You just dropped in your coins and then slide a bottle hanging from the neck to the end of the row and pull it out. The weirdest part was the cooler was not refrigerated; they drank it warm. I tried one once and it tasted terrible. I just couldn't understand hot beer in the middle of summer.

The man who ran the tool department was a very nice Indian who eventually befriended Shorty and me. He even had us to dinner at his apartment one evening where he and his wife served us a chicken dish with rice. He said they knew Americans did not like spicy food the way Indians ate it, so they toned it down for us.

It was the hottest food I had ever had in my life. My mouth was on fire and all they gave us to drink was a tiny amount of wine. We later found out the reason he was so nice to us was that he was trying to get himself and his wife to the U.S. and was hoping in some way that one or both of us could sponsor them. I never felt like we were being used. He was just trying to do what was best for him and his wife.

GERMAN MOVIE THEATER

One time, I went to a German movie theater. We were curious about the fact that movies in Europe were more casual about sex than in the U.S. The movie we watched was not very racy by today's standards, but it did have some sex in it. What was funny was we had no idea of what the story was because of course, it was all in German.

BLACK MARKET PURCHASE

There was a time when Shorty and I both wanted to purchase a brown suede coat. Somehow Shorty found out where we could purchase one at a significant discount. It was on the second floor of a small shop in downtown Heilbronn. Naturally, we went there one Saturday – late afternoon after the shop had closed. I don't recall how we were able to enter the store, but we did and were led upstairs. It felt like we were in an attic.

As we waited to meet with the guy (who appeared to be an old foreigner) that would sell us the coats, we watched him meet with some guy who appeared to be a young immigrant. The old gentleman was seated behind a desk and the young immigrant was standing on the opposite side. They were speaking some foreign language (not German) and when they finished talking the young man went around the desk and they hugged and kissed each other on both cheeks. We felt like it was a scene out of *The Godfather*.

We then met with the old gentleman. He presented us with the coats and subsequently, we tried them on. Both were the correct size, so we made our purchase and were on our way. I had mine for many years and in fact, my late wife Janet loved that coat for some reason. I believe it was the smell of the leather and the style that she liked so much.

CHAPTER FOURTEEN
AUTO RACING

Racing was something Shorty, Kidder, Babich, and I were interested in and we had several opportunities to experience it.

KIDDER AND SHORTY RACING TEAM

Before I went home on leave in 1972, these two got into racing their own car. They found an old VW Beetle, stripped it down, removed the fenders, bumpers, the entire interior except for the driver's seat, and anything else they could remove to make it lighter and faster. They painted it red, white, and blue and numbered it 61, the number of our 5/4-ton motor pool vehicle. They both worked on the car however, Shorty was the driver. I believe they had some success, but I never went to any of their races. I did drive it one time on the motor pool cobblestone area next to the motor pool offices. I do know they had permission from our officers to use a 2-½ ton truck to transport the car. They had fun with it and that is all that mattered.

Kidder burning rubber in his and Shorty's race car. He was down between the truck bays and the wash racks.

HOCKENHEIM RACES

There was a huge racetrack located outside Mannheim called Hockenheim. The cars that raced there were open-wheeled similar to the type of cars that raced at Indy – but not quite as fast. We went only once but it was fun, and we had a good time.

NURBURGRING GRAND PRIX

One of the highlights of seeing a racing event was the German Grand Prix. The cars were Indy-style and just as fast and we had the opportunity to see some very famous drivers at that race such as Emerson Fittipaldi. Interestingly, this track was considered the most dangerous grand Prix track in the world and would eventually be shut down because of too many injuries and deaths.

LE MANS

The most amazing race I ever experienced was the 24-hour race at Le Mans in June of 1973. Babich, Shorty, and I took off early on a Thursday morning in a car we bought just for this race. This same car eventually became the wedding present for Hester and his wife. We traveled the efficient German highways to the border of France and when we crossed into France, we quickly learned that their roads were more like small country roads in the U.S.

It was a beautiful drive along tree-lined country roads and farm fields. We eventually ended up in Paris and although we were only there for a few hours, we were able to visit the Eiffel Tower (we made it to the second tier), went inside Notre Dame, and walked under the Arc de Triumph. Several hours later we drove by the castle at Versailles and it was all lit up. We arrived at Le Mans about midnight and since we had nowhere to stay or sleep, we pulled into a small grocery store parking lot. Since Shorty drove, we let him stretch out in the back of the bug. I slept in the driver's seat and Babich slept in the passenger seat. We looked terrible the next morning – little sleep, unshaven, and unbathed.

We drove around to find food and scope out the town. We saw the original massive Goodyear Blimp which must have been several football fields long. Part of the race track (the fastest part where cars exceed 230 mph) is a regular public road that runs between Le Mans and Tours, France. It is closed off just before the race, but we were able to drive that part of the track on the day we arrived. Eventually, we ended up on a small square plot of land that was just big enough for the car and a tent. That was it! This would be our home until after the race Sunday afternoon. I don't recall what we had to pay to rent the space, but it wasn't cheap.

Shorty, the author, and Babich in front of our car at LeMans.

The race includes three different classes of cars, each of which has its own top speed capability. This makes for a very interesting and challenging race for the drivers since the faster cars can advance on the slower cars very quickly making it difficult to brake or pass.

The entire weekend was like a huge carnival with five hundred thousand folks in attendance. We wandered around Friday afternoon and evening taking it all in. We walked the track and had our picture taken under the famous clock used to track the time. Saturday morning, we arrived at the track when it opened at about 8 AM. We found a spot as close to the starting point as possible and stayed there the entire day as the stands filled up. The race started at 4 PM and would go until 4 PM Sunday.

The author standing under the infamous clock used to track the time of the race.

We watched the beginning of the race at the starting line, then left after about an hour to move to other parts of the track. We watched the race into the night. About 1 AM we went back to our tent and those guys slept very briefly while I slept a few hours longer. I got up the next morning, found the others (don't remember how), and we continued to move to various parts of the track.

We wanted to get to Mulsanne Straight where spectators are not allowed, so we tried acting like photographers when we were stopped by a gendarme (policeman). We tried to fool him, but he figured out that we were just some silly Americans trying to do something we were not allowed to do.

Sunday afternoon after the race ended, we left right away and drove straight back taking a shorter route, however, we still did not get back until about 3 or 4 AM. I don't know how Shorty did it, but he drove the whole way. It was the greatest race I have ever attended.

Prior to this trip, Hester and his new wife were scheduled to arrive at Ramstein Air Base the day we were driving back from Le Mans and so we'd worked out arrangements to pick them up. Somehow, we forgot about this commitment and drove all the way back to Badnerhof instead of heading to Frankfurt first. Poor Hester and Linda waited and waited. When they finally realized we weren't coming they took the train to Heilbronn. However, to this day, I don't understand how we thought we were all going to fit in a VW beetle.

CHAPTER FIFTEEN
STORIES AFTER ROTATING BACK TO THE
STATES (THE WORLD)

A THANKSGIVING FEAST TO REMEMBER

Thanksgiving of 1973 I had just returned home, however, Hester and Kidder were still in Heilbronn. Linda and Hester very nicely had several guys over to dinner for a Thanksgiving feast except it was not your typical turkey dinner. The newlyweds learned that you're supposed to take a frozen turkey out of the freezer three days before cooking so it can thaw, however, they didn't realize that you move it to the refrigerator. Instead, they left it in the sink. By the time it was removed from the wrapper it had spoiled – badly. Hester quickly drove to the commissary, which fortunately was open. Unfortunately, all the turkeys were gone (had there been any they would have been frozen). So instead he purchased several hens. All in all, it sounded like a very successful Thanksgiving feast.

RACIAL TENSION

Unfortunately, racial tension had been brewing a bit while I was there, however, after I was gone, Kidder told me about an incident in the mess hall one morning. Several African

American soldiers were upset about something and according to him began throwing chairs everywhere. Kidder said it got so bad that guys were jumping through the windows to escape. I don't recall the outcome, but I'm sure the MP's were called in at some point. I will say that overall, I got along very well with everyone. I always tried to treat everyone as I liked to be treated, which is what we are all taught in Kindergarten – the Golden Rule.

CQ DUTY AGAIN

Several months after getting out, I was back home and received a letter from Kidder. Included in the letter was a recent Duty Roster and my name was listed as being scheduled for CQ Duty. Needless, to say it no longer applied to me and I had a good laugh about it.

HESTER AND CAPTAIN SPENCER (BATTERY COMMANDER) MEET AGAIN

Interestingly, Hester ran into Spencer on the streets of Washington, DC about 10 years ago who by then was a Colonel. He was responsible for managing something in Washington, but I don't recall what it was. What amazes me, is they recognized one another so many years after they were in A Battery together.

DEADLY ACCIDENT

In 1985, I had been out of the Army for nine years and was reading the newspaper at breakfast when I saw a headline that caught my attention. The article was from Heilbronn, Germany, and was about a Pershing missile accident that had occurred at Redleg training site by C Battery of the 3rd/84th Battalion, 56th Brigade. One of the missile trailers had not been properly grounded, which is necessary to avoid a buildup of static electricity. This electricity caused the missile's fuel to explode which ultimately killed three guys next to the trailer. Another unfortunate accident that should not have happened.

Several years ago, I found an officer on a Pershing Yahoo website who served in A Battery when I was there on active duty. He shared with me that he was still in Pershing when this accident occurred and was given the grisly assignment of ensuring all the remains were collected and accounted for.

I visited that site with my late wife and our daughters in 1997 which by that time was a German park. Within the park was a plaque honoring the three soldiers who gave their lives for the freedom of others. I still have the article to this day.

THE COST OF GETTING MIXED UP WITH DRUGS

Another incident has to do with Nixon, another guy in the motor pool (he's in my motor pool photo above). He loved to claim that everything was bigger in Texas. This particular event occurred after I'd rotated back home but was shared with me by Hester. Nixon's mom was dying of cancer and lived in Dallas but because there was no husband in the picture, Nixon was granted a hardship transfer that would have had him stationed closer to home.

Unfortunately, he got into drugs while in Germany and mistakenly thought he could send drugs home in his gear and that because he was a hardship transfer no one would inspect his gear. He was wrong. They found drugs at Ramstein Airbase in Frankfurt. This was the airport everyone in Europe flew in and out of when going to and from the states. As a result, his friend Hester had to draw a loaded .45 pistol from the armory, travel to Ramstein and in effect bring his friend back to Heilbronn under armed escort. Nixon was required to complete his tour in Germany and he never saw his mom again.

CHAPTER SIXTEEN
ROTATING BACK TO THE STATES

Transferring out is a big deal. Once you get to 99 days remaining with your tour, you're considered a two-digit midget – a short-timer. It's one of the greatest feelings there is. And everyone knows because you have a clipboard with a stack of papers that you carry everywhere. There is a long checklist that must be completed before being processed out of Germany and ultimately reassigned to Fort Dix, New Jersey.

The checklist requires you to go to many different offices, establishments, etc., and obtain signoff from each that you don't have any outstanding debts or other unresolved matters that would be considered unfinished business before you leave. This required me to visit places at Badnerhof Kaserne, Wharton Barracks, and Neckarsulm Kaserne. By this time, Babich had left in August and Shorty had left in September. Hester and Kidder still had about six months before they would rotate back to the states.

A GIFT

Just before I left, the guys in the motor pool gave me a gift. It was a lighter with "to Sgt Heyer from the Motor Pool Men" engraved on one side. I was very touched by this kind act. It really meant a lot to me and I still have this lighter today.

GOING HOME

The day I left was very surreal. As I stated earlier, I had been a part of this unit for more than two and a half years, then all of a sudden, I was leaving. Being disconnected like that was a very odd feeling. I no longer felt like I was part of this group and that feeling had a profound impact on me. I was so happy to be going home, yet so sad to be leaving what had become my normal life.

Hester and Kidder drove me to Ramstein Air Base for the flight back to Fort Dix, New Jersey via McGuire Air Force Base. When I arrived at Fort Dix, I was left with the impression that it would take a couple of days to rotate out, but it did not take more than a day maybe two. When the paperwork was processed, I received eight brand new crisp 100-dollar bills as payout for the leave days I never used.

I was issued a plane ticket, placed on a bus to Philadelphia, and headed that way. I caught my plane to St. Louis and when I arrived, I could not believe I was back home. I called my brother Rick and waited outside for him to pick me up. He arrived with his girlfriend Denise whom I'd never met. I was on cloud nine. It was the greatest moment in my life up until that time.

RETURNING TO CIVILIAN LIFE

A week after I completed my tour of duty, I was already back working at Tom's gas station where I'd worked part-time before I entered the Army. In that first week, I met my first wife Janet when she randomly came in to get gas for her parent's car. Thanks to her, she convinced me to return to college and so I did, enrolling at the University of Missouri, St. Louis in the fall of 1974. Using the GI Bill, I graduated in three and a half years with a BSBA in Finance. I would later obtain an MBA in Finance from Webster University – graduating with honors. Thanks to her and the faith she had in me I earned two degrees I never thought I would earn.

My first job after graduating from the University of Missouri, St. Louis with my undergraduate degree was with LaBarge, Inc. The company traded on the AMEX (American Stock Exchange). I had several accounting jobs with them – Corporate Accountant and Assistant Controller with a subsidiary. After 4 ½ years with them, I was hired by Anheuser-Busch, Co's, Inc. I started there as a staff accountant in the Controller's Group working my way up to Accounting Manager. I was there for almost 27 years, retiring in 2008. During my career, A-B was a Fortune 50 Company and one of those years was voted #1 best place to work in America.

VISITING HEILBRONN IN 1997

In 1997, I was fortunate enough to visit Heilbronn with my late wife Janet and my two daughters – Jenny and Megan. We spent a couple of days there and re-visited many sites that I have discussed previously. Interestingly, we had rented a car and I was able to drive around for the most part and find places with little or no difficulty even though I had been gone for 24 years.

Badnerhof Kaserne was gone and was now just a vacant field with a fence around it. This site is now a subdivision that I discovered because I have been able to find it on Google Maps sitting at the comfort of my PC in my own home approximately 4,600 miles away. I'm able to make out the outline of what once was the compound in which I lived.

Wharton Barracks was in the process of being demolished. However, the officer and NCO housing adjacent to the barracks was now low-income housing for refugees. Neckarsulm Kaserne was also low-income housing for refugees. Redleg as mentioned previously had been turned into a German park with what appeared to be walking trails. All of these changes came about because of the Iraq War. Most units from Germany were transferred to Kuwait in preparation for the war, resulting in Germany repatriating these facilities.

Horten's – the downtown department store was still there. In fact, Janet and my daughters each purchased a necklace from there as a souvenir and we had our picture taken in front of the store. The park just down the road from Badnerhof where I attended rock concerts was still there too.

It was very surreal to visit these places with my family. On the one hand, it was very sad to see what had become of all of these places that played a role in my life during my years in the Army. Yet it was also so much fun to see these places with my family and for me to try and bring them to life for them.

MAKING A HOME IN EUROPE

I know of at least two instances where guys stayed in Europe on a longer-term basis.

Connors made the Army a career and spent almost all of his time in the Army stationed in Germany. He married a German girl and after he got out, he moved back to Buffalo which is where he is originally from.

About 12 years ago, I found an email group on Yahoo that was comprised of folks that served in the Pershing Missile Program. I participated for a couple of years but lost interest after Janet passed. During that time, however, I befriended a guy (Harris) who had been assigned to B Battery while I was in A Battery next door. He did not make the Army a career, but he did marry an Austrian girl and built a life with her in Austria.

STRESS ON THE JOB

While on Yahoo, I connected with a guy (Saunders) who was an officer over one of A Battery's firing platoons and was a young college graduate, about 25, during the time I was in A Battery. He shared with me that while he was over a firing platoon that his stomach was always in knots. His stress was because he knew the capabilities of the missiles and recognized the overwhelming responsibility he carried having three missiles under his command.

SPEAKING WITH HIGH SCHOOL KIDS

About twelve years ago a friend of mine from my church, retired Major Jones (a man who is a class act), connected me with a group of veterans that speak at Kirkwood High School. Shortly thereafter, I began speaking at Webster and Lindbergh's High Schools as well. I also spoke at Clayton High School, but that was more recent and lasted for just two years. Each program is different, but the goal of each is the same: to share our individual stories with the students to help bring history to life.

I love speaking with the students. I inform them that serving in the Army taught me discipline, teamwork, and leadership. Skills that have served me well throughout my life. They are very interested in what we have to share and ask great questions. I have a PowerPoint presentation that I use that contains approximately 20 slides of photos that I display as I go through my talking points. I love to ask if any of the kids in the room are 18 since that's how old I was when I enlisted. I'm able to add to the realism of my experience because I can still fit into my class A's dress uniform that was issued to me almost 50 years ago. The other veterans love to give me a hard time because many of them are unable to do so.

The other wonderful part of this program is the veterans get to hear stories of other veterans. I have heard amazing stories of bravery, self-sacrifice, honor, and duty. A number of these guys were wounded in combat. I have a great deal of respect for those who served in a combat zone – WWII, the Korean War, or Vietnam. These guys and those that did not return home are the true heroes. They deserve everyone's respect and gratitude.

Don't get me wrong. I am very proud of my service to my country. I consider my enlistment in the Army patriotic. However, those that served in the military in a combat zone are the heroes. And especially the ones that made the ultimate sacrifice.

Interestingly, one of the guys that I speak with (Lt Little) was an officer in the Army. He did serve in Vietnam and was responsible for overseeing truck convoys that were used to deliver supplies to outlying bases and posts. Before serving in Vietnam, he was stationed at Neckarsulm Kaserne a couple of years before I arrived in Germany. Just another one of the connections that I always find interesting. After Vietnam, I believe he rarely spoke of his experiences until he started speaking to high school students.

This is probably a little-known fact, but combat infantry makes up only about 15% of soldiers in a war zone. In other words, there are approximately 5-6 support soldiers for every combat soldier.

OTHER CONNECTIONS

Another interesting connection I discovered about 10 years ago was with an assistant priest at my church. Her father-in-law was in Army Intelligence in the 1950s and was also stationed at Badnerhof Kaserne before it became a part of the Pershing Missile Program.

Once I was having my oil changed (yes – after about 15 years of working on my own cars, I stopped). I was sitting in the waiting room and a gentleman about my age saw my "Army Veteran" hat and asked when I was in. This is generally how conversations with other vets get started. Anyway, I explained when I was in and that I served in Germany. We then figured out we were in at the same time. He was in the infantry in Germany and was assigned to the 3rd/84th field artillery. Ultimately, he would pull guard duty at Kleingartach. He told me about a time when they caught a spy outside the compound but in the area.

ON THE OTHER SIDE

While working at Anheuser-Busch, I made many friends. However, one noteworthy friendship was with a Russian (A.A.) who emigrated to the U.S. to find a better life for himself and his family.

During one of those times when you are sharing some of your personnel life, we determined his older brother served in the Russian Army at the same time I was serving in Germany. His brother was in a missile unit (surface to air and surface to ground). It was not a nuclear missile unit, but just as our missiles were pointed at Russian targets in a defensive position, their missiles were also pointed in our direction in a defensive position. His brother achieved the rank of sergeant just as I had.

LOSS OF A PIONEER

I have an article from the *St. Louis Post-Dispatch* dated 05/13/2010, that indicates Edward Uhl (formerly of St. Louis) helped invent the Bazooka during WWII to counter German Panzers. Later, in 1947 he joined the Glenn L. Martin Co., where he eventually led the development of the Pershing I missile, capable of carrying a nuclear warhead.

DEFCON 3

During the Arab/Israeli War of October 1973, Pershing units in Germany went to DEFCON 3 to scare the Soviets and keep them out of the Middle East...we know it worked because we lived through it.

CHAPTER SEVENTEEN
END OF THE PERSHING MISSILE PROGRAM

The Pershing Program continued after I rotated back home. Pershing 1a Missiles were replaced by Pershing II Missiles. The rollout began in 1983 and was fully functional by December 1985. The warheads were less deadly than the 1a missiles, but the range of the II's was substantially further than their predecessor. As a result, the Pershing program now had the capability to reach Russian soil. This got the attention of the Russians rather quickly who had previously not been too serious about negotiating a treaty with regard to nuclear-based ground missiles.

Below is a story that I have in my military file that emphasizes the risks the Pershing Missile program had created.

"I came across an interesting story while researching the Pershing 1a...So the story went, in 1983 NATO was conducting a nuclear readiness exercise. Unbeknownst to the NATO leaders the Soviets had changed their response policy from fire on launch of NATO weapons to one of fire on SUSPICION of launch due to the fact that Pershing 2's based in Germany would reach command centres in Moscow about the same time they had confirmation of a launch. Accordingly, the Soviets stepped up their espionage in the U.S.

Originally, both Reagan and Bush Sr. were to participate in the exercise but officials felt that this would be "provocative" and the exercise went ahead without their direct participation. As the exercise began the Soviets raised their readiness to the highest level as they could not be sure that this wasn't a cover for a first strike by NATO. The earliest indication of an actual launch by NATO would be a burst of radio traffic but the standing down of the NATO nuclear forces would also generate a similar burst of radio traffic. The Soviets were panicked, many argued if they didn't launch now they'd never have a chance to do it. They consulted their agents in Washington and they reported that Reagan was at a public function and the Doves argued that the U.S. would have Reagan in a shelter if they were going to launch a first strike. American officials had a similar problem as they were aware of Soviet readiness to launch and were afraid to stand down their forces. It seems kind of like two gunfighters waiting for the twitch that the other was about to draw.

Reagan was hustled from the banquet back to the White House and got on the hotline with Gorbachev. They negotiated the stand down of the nukes and the crisis was over. We can speculate about what else they said but it is revealing that not long afterward talks were scheduled on reducing nuclear weapons and the first to go were the Pershing missiles."

Through these negotiations, the INF treaty (Intermediate-Range Nuclear Forces Treaty) was eventually signed by both the

U.S. and the Soviet Union on May 8, 1987. It took several years after the signing to completely dismantle the missiles and destroy the warheads. A team of Soviet representatives oversaw our program, and the U.S. had a team that oversaw the mutual destruction of the Soviet ground missiles. The last active Pershing Missile was destroyed in May 1991.

In addition, the Pershing program (II precisely) has been credited with ending the Cold War and bringing down the Berlin wall in November 1991. That is an amazing accomplishment considering how long the Soviet Union had been in existence – essentially since the end of WWI. And construction on the Berlin wall began in 1961.

Today there are two remaining Pershing II Missiles on display alongside a Russian-made nuclear missile. One pair is located at the Air and Space Museum (in the entrance) in Washington, DC. The other pair is located in a museum in Moscow, Russia.

Note: sadly, during the entire Pershing Missile Program 56 Pershing Missile military personnel lost their lives serving in the line of duty. This sobering statistic reminds me of the song by Crosby, Stills, Nash and Young "Find the Cost of Freedom." There is a particular verse that always strikes a chord with me. "Find the cost of freedom buried in the ground. Mother earth will swallow you lay your body down." Finally, others died as well, such as Griffon and Crown in the auto accident. So, the actual number of deaths was higher than the officially reported deaths of 56 who died in the line of duty.

In 1992, the Iraqi War took place. Many if not most of the troops for that war came from the troops stationed in Germany. As such, there was a huge drawdown of troops in that country at that time.

2010 REUNION

In April of 2010, we held a reunion. Babich, Gacek (Shorty), Hester, Kidder, and I met in Charleston, West Virginia. Charleston was selected because it was the most central city for all of us. Gacek (Shorty) and Kidder's wives also attended. I brought my photo albums and Babich brought his 8mm movies. It was as though we had never been apart even though all of us had not been together since 1973.

We spent the weekend telling stories and laughing. It was wonderful. The bond we had formed 38 years prior to the reunion was as strong as ever. Recently, we began planning another reunion. Unfortunately, CV-19 interrupted our plans. So even though they are temporarily on hold, plans will resume when life returns somewhat to normal. And this time we all plan to bring our wives, so they can hear our boring stories and commiserate with one another.

Back row: Brenda Kidder, Randy Hester.
Middle row: Barry Kidder, Sue Gacek, Andy (Shorty) Gacek
Front row: the author and John (Bahko) Babich

I love these guys and am so proud that I served with them.

EPILOGUE

I have been wanting for more than 20 years to document my time in the military. Initially, the primary reason was to share my story with my family – wife, children, grandchildren, etc., and possibly a few close friends. However, as I began to recall my training and all the stories I wanted to share, I began to recognize that my story was not special in any way. But rather a retelling of what any soldier might have experienced that served in Europe as part of the NATO forces in the early 1970s. At that time, there was approximately 250,000 combined U.S. Army and Air Force military personnel stationed in Europe.

In 2011, my beloved wife of 34 ½ years passed away after a brief illness. I was devastated. I joined a grief group, just one of several measures I took, to cope with my loss. And even though the last thing I ever thought was that I would meet another woman, I did. I met a wonderful lady, Joan, whose husband had passed away the previous year. In time, we fell in love and married in 2016.

POSTSCRIPT

Recently (July 16, 2020), I came across three editorials in the *St. Louis Post-Dispatch* that are somewhat related to my story. The first was an OP-ED by Mark Hertling a retired lieutenant general who commanded U.S. Army, Europe, in 2012.

It states the U.S. military bases serve vital support functions across continents. While U.S. troops in Germany were once the largest part of a NATO deterrent to the Soviet Union during the Cold War, the mission has transformed over the last three decades. While the U.S. had over a quarter-million troops in Europe until 1990, we now have 30,000 soldiers and about 20,000 airmen there. The mission may have changed, but our presence in that part of the world is still relevant even today.

The next editorial (by the *Post-Dispatch* editorial board) recognizes that July 16, 2020, was the 75th anniversary of the birth of the nuclear era. Splitting the atom was the earth-shaking event that ended WWII, launched the Cold War, provided an international arms race that continues today, and sparked the quest by more and more countries to gain entry to the club of nuclear superpowers. Americans must never lose sight of the awesome destructive power at the fingertips of a tiny number of leaders around the world. As such, this nation's choice of leaders matters greatly.

The final editorial (by the *Post-Dispatch* editorial board) notes that vesting sole control over nukes in one person is insanity. It must change. Many Americans may not know it, but the nation's entire nuclear arsenal can be launched by one person – the president – at any time, for any reason, with no input from anyone else. "Presidents, like all of us, make mistakes. They are only human," writes former U.S. Defense Secretary William Perry.

In a new book he co-authored, he writes, "It is time to retire the nuclear button. No one should have the unchecked power to destroy the world." The current system of total presidential control began under the first president of the nuclear age, Harry Truman, out of fear overzealous generals might use this terrifying new weapon unnecessarily. Also, the rationale that the authority is vested only with the president because there would not be sufficient time to consult with Congress is no longer true.

The author's suggestion for avoiding a presidential mistake includes an ironclad U.S. policy against launching a first strike; a designated group from Congress that must agree to <u>any</u> nuclear launch, and retiring all land-based (as opposed to submarine-based) missiles – thus removing that tempting target for a would-be attacker, ensuring the president isn't forced into "a quick 'use-them-or-lose-them' decision."

ACKNOWLEDGEMENTS

I would like to thank the following individuals for their contributions to this memoir. Additional stories and clarification with others provided by John Babich, Andy Gacek, Randy Hester, and Barry Kidder. The bond we formed in the Army has endured and will last until we are all gone. Editing and wordsmithing by my daughter Jenny Medenwald – an accomplished author. Words cannot express my gratitude for your expertise in making this a better story. It was a joy to work with you. Additional review by Lyn Ballard another author and a good friend. I also obtained input from my good friends Vicki and Jim Erwin – both authors. Re-typing assistance by my wife Joan Sale Heyer. You made the project much easier. What a wonderful partner you are – thank you. And overall support from Joan Sale Heyer, my daughters Jenny Medenwald and Megan Baird, and the rest of my immediate family – Dallas Medenwald, Adam Baird, Mike and Sara Sale, and Jaclyn and Greg Pillar, and my six plus grandchildren. I'm eternally grateful to all of these individuals for their friendship, love, and support. Thank you.

ABOUT THE AUTHOR

Mike Heyer enlisted shortly after entering college and four months after graduating from high school. He signed up for three years (volunteered) for the U.S. Army during the Cold War with Russia and the Vietnam War, which was still being fought in Southeast Asia.

He would complete basic training and AIT (Advanced Individual Training) for mechanics school – both at Fort Leonard Wood. His permanent station assignment would take him to West Germany where he was assigned to the only nuclear missile unit in the U.S. Army – the Pershing Missile System. Interestingly, it was considered intermediate field artillery. He was ultimately assigned to the 56th Brigade, 3rd Battalion 84th Field Artillery – "A" Battery of the famed 7th Army.

This experience had a powerful and positive impact on his life that still affects him to this day. After completing his tour, he met and married the love of his life, had two beautiful daughters, and went on to earn a college degree and an MBA both in finance. He would spend his professional career working as an accountant for two major corporations working in a variety of positions.

He's proud of his service to his country and the fine men in this memoir with whom he has had the honor to serve. He remains friends to this day with several of his army buddies. A lifelong bond that never fades.

Mike is now retired and has remarried to another wonderful woman after his first wife passed away in 2011 following a brief illness. He volunteers his time with several organizations, is a runner, plays golf, hikes, bikes, reads, travels, and spends time with his children and grandchildren.

BIBLIOGRAPHY

Some material came from or provided by the following resources:

Additional material provided by an article titled "The Army's Precision 'Sunday Punch', by Kaulene Hughes, October 2009." Where the article was published is unknown.

The first atom is split:
https://en.wikipedia.org/wiki/Ernest_Rutherford

The first atomic detonation:
https://en.wikipedia.org/wiki/Trinity_(nuclear_test)

Construction on the Berlin Wall was found at the following website: https://en.wikipedia.org/wiki/Berlin_Wall

The date the Berlin wall came down was found on the following website: https://en.wikipedia.org/wiki/Fall_of_the_Berlin_Wall

C5 Galaxy Photo found at:
https://upload.wikimedia.org/wikipedia/commons/thumb/e/e6/C5_galaxy.jpg/120px-C5_galaxy.jpg

C-5 Galaxy Airplane specs:
https://en.wikipedia.org/wiki/Lockheed_C-5_Galaxy

Details of the Chinook crash in 1971 located at the following website: https://www.nytimes.com/1971/08/19/archives/37-g-is-killed-as-copter-crashes-in-west-germany.html

CH47 Chinook photo found at the following website:
https://upload.wikimedia.org/wikipedia/commons/c/c5/D103_CH47_Chinook_KLU_%287267199490%29.jpg

214 · MICHAEL W HEYER

CH 47 Chinook Helicopter specs:
https://en.wikipedia.org/wiki/Boeing_CH-47_Chinook

Additional material provided by:
https://en.wikipedia.org/wiki/The_Cold_War_Museum

F4 Phantom photo found at:
https://upload.wikimedia.org/wikipedia/commons/thumb/2/2b/QF-4_Holloman_AFB.jpg/120px-QF-4_Holloman_AFB.jpg

F4 Phantom specs:
https://www.google.com/search?q=f4+phantom+jet+specs&rlz=1C1CHBF_enUS887US887&oq=f4+phantom+jet+specs&aqs=chrome..69i57j0l5.8458j0j7&sourceid=chrome&ie=UTF-8

Fort Leonard Wood WWII barracks photo:
https://www.google.com/search?rlz=1C1CHBF_enUS887US887&source=univ&tbm=isch&q=what+did+WWII+barracks+look+like+at+ft+leonard+wood+look+like&sa=X&ved=2ahUKEwjnmYWBpPDqAhUQ16wKHTU4AfUQsAR6BAgGEAE&biw=1280&bih=610

Fort Leonard Wood Newer barracks photo - basic training:
https://www.google.com/search?rlz=1C1CHBF_enUS887US887&ei=s0kgX4j2L8LysQXYgpCwCQ&q=brick+building+barracks+at+fort+leonard+wood+in+the+1970%27s&oq=brick+building+barracks+at+fort+leonard+wood+in+the+1970%27s&gs_lcp=CgZwc3ktYWIQAzoECAAQRzoFCAAQzQI6BAghEApQvb8BWKybAmCrowJoAHACeACAAYYBiAGoHZIBBTE3LjE5mAEAoAEBqgEHZ3dzLXdpcesABAQ&sclient=psy-ab&ved=0ahUKEwjIm-7kpvDqAhVCeawKHVgBBJYQ4dUDCAw&uact=5

German weather provided by:
https://en.wikipedia.org/wiki/List_of_cities_by_average_temperature

Google Earth - Viewing a satellite image from space was the following website: https://en.wikipedia.org/wiki/Google_Earth

Information regarding the mining of Haiphong Harbor in North Vietnam can be found on the following website: https://en.wikipedia.org/wiki/Operation_Pocket_Money

Bell UH-1Huey Helicopter specs: https://en.wikipedia.org/wiki/Bell_UH-1_Iroquois

The signing date of the INF treaty was found on the following website: https://en.wikipedia.org/wiki/Intermediate-Range_Nuclear_Forces_Treaty

Insignias - Pershing Patch: https://www.google.com/search?q=Pershing+missile+patch&rlz=1C1CHBF_enUS887US887&oq=Pershing+missile+patch&aqs=chrome..69i57.4799j0j4&sourceid=chrome&ie=UTF-8

Insignias - Seventh Army: https://en.wikipedia.org/wiki/Seventh_United_States_Army

M16 photo found at: https://commons.wikimedia.org/wiki/File:M16duckbill.gif

M16 specifications were found at the following website: https://en.wikipedia.org/wiki/M16_rifle

M60 Patton Tank photo: https://www.google.com/url?sa=i&url=https%3A%2F%2Fcommons.wikimedia.org%2Fwiki%2FFile%3AM60_Patton_%2527Patton_Tank%2527_P5250358.JPG&psig=AOvVaw2YG6cKZUSQBciQ5kMLypyo&ust=1601826994685000&source=images&cd=vfe&ved=2ahUKEwje1azZ5JjsAhVIbK0KHQzACGkQr4kDegUIARC3Ag

M60 Patton Tank specs: https://en.wikipedia.org/wiki/M60_tank

The Manhattan Project: https://en.wikipedia.org/wiki/Manhattan_Project

Map of Germany from the following website: https://www.google.com/search?rlz=1C1CHBF_enUS887US887&source=univ&tbm=isch&q=2009+google+map+of+germany

&sa=X&ved=2ahUKEwiOppyg4KLqAhXbZs0KHVnZCMQQ7Al6BAgIEBk&biw=1280&bih=610

Medals - Army Commendation Medal:
https://veteranmedals.army.mil/awardg&d.nsf/%24%24OpenDominoDocument.xsp?documentId=5AB894DA035BADAF85256B660063F3A8&action=editDocument

Medals - Good Conduct Medal:
https://www.usamm.com/products/army-good-conduct-medal-ribbon

Medals - Medal of Honor:
https://en.wikipedia.org/wiki/Medal_of_Honor

Medals - National Defense Medal:
https://www.medalsofamerica.com/blog/national-defense-service-medal-blog-post/

Medals - Pershing QRA Badge:
https://en.wikipedia.org/wiki/Pershing_Professionals_Badge

Medals - Sharpshooter, Marksman and Expert badges:
https://www.military.com/join-armed-forces/army-weapons-qualification-course.html

Military Justice - Information regarding an Article 15 in the Army can be found at the following website:
https://www.justia.com/military-law/military-criminal-justice-system/article-15/

Monuments Men the movie:
https://www.google.com/search?gs_ssp=eJzj4tLP1TfIS6kwLioxYPTiyc3PK81NzStRABIAcPEIzQ&q=monument+men&rlz=1C1CHBF_enUS887US887&oq=monument+men&aqs=chrome.1.69i57j46j0l6.5946j1j8&sourceid=chrome&ie=UTF-8

NATO forces in Europe in the early 1970's was found on the following website:
https://en.wikipedia.org/wiki/History_of_NATO

Nike and Kleingartach: http://charlie3rd71st.com/

When the nuclear arms race began:
https://en.wikipedia.org/wiki/Nuclear_arms_race

The Oath of Enlisment was found at the following website:
https://www.military.com/join-armed-forces/swearing-in-for-military-service.html

Pershing Cycles - Reprinted with permission from Walter Gates (PTS Operator, Charlie Battery, 3rd Platoon, 3/84th FA Neckarsulm, 1973-1974.

Information regarding the Pershing Missile explosion at Redleg was from the "*St. Louis Post-Dispatch* – Sunday, January 13, 1985 page 3A – Inquiry Started Into Missile Fire."

The history of the Pershing Missile Systems was found at the following website: https://history.redstone.army.mil/miss-pershing.html

Credit for the Pershing Missile Program ending the Cold War and bringing down the Berlin wall was provided by "Forty Autumns: A Family's Story of Courage and Survival on Both Sides of the Berlin Wall by Nina Willner, copyright 2016."

The dates of when A Battery fired test rockets at Cape Canaveral in February 1973 located at the following website: http://afspacemuseum.org/library/histories/Army.pdf

When the first Pershing II Missiles were placed in service was located on the following website:
https://en.wikipedia.org/wiki/Pershing_II

The date of the destruction of the last active Pershing Missile was found on the following website:
https://en.wikipedia.org/wiki/Pershing_II

The number of servicemen and women who died in the line of duty provided by:
https://history.army.mil/armyhistory/AH73(W).pdf

Loss of a Pioneer from an article from the *St. Louis Post-Dispatch* dated 05/13/2010.

Video of the Pershing Missile Program was found at the following website:
https://www.youtube.com/watch?v=x7YABPisFGE

Risks - How long we had to live after firing our missiles provided by:
https://www.usarmygermany.com/Units/FieldArtillery/USAREUR_56th%20FA%20Bde.htm

The story of the "Risks of the Pershing Missile Program" provided by a document I have in my file, source, and date unknown.

Information regarding Stars and Stripes provided by:
https://www.loc.gov/rr/main/stars/intro.html#:~:text=On%20November%209%2C%201861%2C%20the,newspaper%20was%20Stars%20and%20Stripes%20

St. Louis Post-Dispatch editorials can be found in the July 16, 2020 copy of the *St. Louis Post-Dispatch*.

Uriah Heep the band:
https://en.wikipedia.org/wiki/Uriah_Heep_(band)#:~:text=Uriah%20Heep%20released%20their%2023rd,He%20was%2062%20years%20old.

Vehicles - M757 tractor and M791 specifications were found at the following website: https://en.wikipedia.org/wiki/M656

Made in the USA
Monee, IL
19 April 2021